## RUGBY LEA
*After a Lo...  ...ur*

© Tom Mather

The moral rights of Tom Mather as the author have been identified.

This book is copy right under the Berne Convention. All rights are reserved. It is sold subject to the condition that it shall not by way of trade or otherwise, be lent, resold, hired out or otherwise circulated without the publisher's prior consent in any form of binding or cover other than that in which it is published and without a similar condition being imposed on the subsequent purchaser. The book shall not be electronically transmitted to another person or persons.

The author has not intentionally breached any copyright or libeled any individual(s) in producing this book. Should anyone feel the author has done so if they contact the author, he will happily alter the wording.

Tom Mather  2021

# RUGBY LEAGUE IS BORN
## *After a Long Labour*

### ACKNOWLEDGEMENTS

There are a number of people who made significant contributions to this book not least are Terry Williams the Australian rugby league historian. Also, John Coffey the New Zealand rugby league journalist, writer and historian. Both were kind enough to read the manuscript and comment on the work. Equally the Huddersfield Rugby League Heritage site provided a good deal of information with regard to George Boak. While the information is in the public domain it did provide an excellent starting point for further research into George Boak.

My thanks go to the reporters of the following newspapers that are referenced in the book:-

The Athletic News Annual 1895-96, Birmingham Daily Post, The Daily Telegraph, Edinburgh Daily Mail, The Gloucester Citizen, The Hartlepools Times, The Huddersfield Chronicle, The Hull Daily Mail, The Leeds Mercury, The Leeds Times, The Liverpool Mercury, The Manchester Courier, The Press (New Zealand), The Sheffield Daily Telegraph, The Sunday Times, The Yorkshire Evening Post, The York Herald, The Western Mail.

*Rugby League is Born*

# CONTENTS

## INTRODUCTION

### Chapter One - (1892)

### Chapter Two - (1893)

### Chapter Three - (1894)

### Chapter Four - (1895)

### Chapter Five - (The Meeting)

### Chapter Six - (Conclusions)

**Appendix One - (George Boak)**

**Appendix Two - (Senior Competition Shield)**

**Appendix Three - (Tony Fattorini)**

# INTRODUCTION

A great deal has been written over the last one hundred and twenty-six years. Some of it very recently regarding the actions of the twenty-one rugby club representatives who established the Northern Union, now the Rugby League, way back in August 1895. Many believe the schism from the parent body the Rugby Union was inevitable and have put forward sociological reasons for this, along with psychological explanations.

The sociological differences were cited as being the financial differences that existed between the wealthy south of the country and the poorer working class industrial north. The view was that the game was played in the south predominantly by those in private schools, universities and old boys clubs set up by those who had attended the former establishments. In the north, clubs tended to be made up of working-class young men who laboured in the mills, mines, factories and engineering establishments. At that time their working week involved five and a half days, they generally ended their working week around noon if not later on a Saturday.

This meant they often barely had time to get to their club to play the game. If they wanted to play in an away game for their club they needed to leave their place of work early. Such action was looked upon by their employer in a not so philanthropic way. In truth they reduced the players wages thus disadvantaging the player financially. The clubs simply made up the wages the player had lost.

The view in the north was that players simply could not afford to play the game without such financial help from their clubs. While in the south the view was if you could not afford to play the game then do not play.

From a psychological point of view the authorities in the south in particular and the clubs in the south in general were less than happy with the way the game was played in the north. Players in the north did not play the game in the right spirit; it was felt the northern players played the game up to and often beyond the rules. In other words, they did not play the game for the games sake they played to win. This as was stated was frowned upon by clubs and officials in the south. This viewpoint is difficult to reconcile as when an England team was selected it contained players from both the north and the south. Surely the varying players did not have or play with differing views and spirits when representing England.

It is not the intention of this book to prove or disprove these differing somewhat academic explanations for the breakaway. It is merely the aim to provide perhaps a more down to earth if somewhat controversial explanation for the reader. It looks to do this by examining newspaper accounts of the events that took place in the lead up to that fateful meeting, at the George Hotel. Of course, the fact that newspaper reports could well be biased for or against a particular viewpoint back then needs also to be considered. The reader must make up their own mind as to whether the official account of events from the authorities back in 1895 and still maintained today is correct. Or, do the newspaper articles contained in this book controversially cast doubts on this so-called official account. Certainly, the official view and one which is maintained to this day is that the dispute centred solely around the issue of broken time and such payments being made to players. It is the author's contention that such a view is not strictly true but was contrived by those involved at the time of the split in an attempt to curry favour with a rugby world which was totally at odds with the actions of the senior clubs.

The differences that occurred took differing forms in Lancashire and Yorkshire but were concentrated initially not on broken time but rather promotion and relegation on merit. That occurred normally in Lancashire not so in Yorkshire. In Lancashire there was also the more sinister claim of professionalism which led to clubs being suspended and an attempt to make the senior competition in the county fully professional. Secondly, there was a demand by the clubs to be in control of their own destiny a demand in which authorities were never going to agree.

## CHAPTER ONE

## (1892)

There are very few supporters of the game of rugby league who do not have just an inkling of how the game originated. The story of its inception that has been embellished and supported over time tell us of the dispute between the new code and the established rugby union authorities. We are told that the game had its origins in a now famous meeting on Thursday, 29th August 1895, at the George Hotel in Huddersfield West Yorkshire.

So, the story goes, twenty one senior rugby club representatives from Lancashire and Yorkshire met that evening to discuss the intransigent attitude of the rugby union authorities to the issue of 'broken time payments' made to players. These were payments that were made to players who had to leave their place of work early in order that they might play for their club. In doing so they lost wages and the clubs simply made up the wages the players had lost. These payments had been made to players for perhaps ten or fifteen years or more albeit illegally.

However, in 1893 the Rugby Union authorities had tightened up the rules on professionalism. The result of this was that clubs in the North of England were being fined or suspended when it was found they had paid broken-time. We are told that after a long discussion it was decided that the clubs would not be able to alter the intransigent attitude of the Rugby Union to these payments. Consequently, the decision was made to resign from the Rugby Union, form their own Northern Union, make their own laws and pay broken-time.

The question is a simple one, is this what really happened or were there other factors which forced the decision on those twenty one clubs to break away from the Rugby Union. The evidence albeit from newspaper reports of the time suggests that this was the case and also it has to be said it was not the first time the senior clubs in Yorkshire had resigned from the rugby union game. In order to get some idea of the events that led to the break away one needs to go back in time but not to 1895, rather we need to go back to 1877. That was the first time the Yorkshire Cup was played for the importance of this event was that it was competitive rugby. While frowned upon by the game's authorities based in London it was allowed to go ahead.

In 1884 the clubs in West Lancashire took the decision to form themselves into a Union. So it was that the West Lancashire Union was formed. Just one year later they also introduced a cup competition on similar lines to the Yorkshire Cup. Just four short years later they abandoned that cup competition and replaced it with a 'League' competition. The authorities telling reporters that such a move would **'spread the excitement throughout the whole of the season'**. So, as the 1890s arrived in the North of England competitive cup and league rugby was an established fact.

Things were however, far from well within the game particularly with the senior clubs in Lancashire and more particularly Yorkshire. At the end of the 1891-92 season matters came to a head. It was the Yorkshire clubs that were facing enormous problems and those problems were presenting themselves on two fronts. Firstly, there was the alarming drop off in the number of supporters coming through the turn stiles to watch games. If the club was playing in a Yorkshire Cup match or a local derby then a good crowd was assured. On the other hand, the mundane week in and week out bread and butter games were increasingly being viewed as meaningless. Consequently, the supporters were staying away in ever increasing numbers and that spelled financial disaster for the clubs.

The second problem came from the rival code of Association Football, by the end of the 1891-92 season that Association was successfully running two divisions. Each of those divisions was made up of sixteen clubs all of whom were increasing their fan base year on year. That also spelled financial ruin for senior clubs. It was obvious that something had to be done to stem the tide. It was a similar story with the game in Lancashire as soccer was presenting major problems perhaps due to the fact that a great many of those clubs were plying their trade in the first division and attracting more and more supporters away from rugby. Sadly, there was a fly in the ointment with regard to rugby clubs and it was from a man in the midst of those northern clubs.

The authorities in London had for some time been growing more and more alarmed with what they perceived was happening to the game in the North of England. It was something of an open secret that clubs were paying broken-time to players in contravention of the rules of the game. That being the case the Reverend Frank Marshall had taken it upon himself to rid the game of the evils of professionalism. To him the major problem stemmed from the increase in competitive games via cup and league rugby. He began to work tirelessly to root out professional acts made by clubs or players.

Sadly, the authorities in London threw their full support behind Marshall's efforts, unlike the football authorities who took a more pragmatic view. When in 1885 the 'Football League' had stated that they were professional, the Football Association simply accepted the decision and the code moved forward. Rugby clubs in the north had watched on enviously at this attitude to professional football and moved their efforts underground. The problem was that clubs were desperately trying to become more and more successful. More success meant greater gates which meant greater financial clout which in turn lead to the ability to buy more success. It was a vicious circle which was growing in complexity.

Clubs were poaching players from other clubs by offering incentives which again were against the rules of the game. A generous club benefactor would find employment for a player who agreed to move to the club. After games players would find cash had been placed in their jacket pocket particularly if they had won the game. It was a system which was becoming increasingly difficult to keep underground particularly as Marshall was constantly turning up at clubs to investigate claims made against officials and players. In spite of all these efforts supporters were still growing tired of watching what they saw as mundane meaningless games.

The problem the clubs faced was that they needed to serve two masters. On a day-to-day basis they were subject to the rules imposed upon them by the Yorkshire County Rugby Union authorities. While on a broader basis they needed to comply to the wishes of the Rugby Union authorities who were firmly based in London. The clubs felt they had no other option but to take proactive action. Also, the decision was made initially by clubs to act in secret and so ten Yorkshire clubs arrange to meet at a location in Leeds. Those ten clubs were Bradford, Leeds, Huddersfield, Halifax, Dewsbury, Hunslet, Liversedge, Brighouse, Batley and Wakefield.

The intention was to set up an Alliance League on similar lines to that adopted by the West Lancashire Union back in 1889 but the problems they faced turned out to be threefold. Firstly, when the plan leaked out other clubs in the county were quite resentful feeling they also should have been included. Secondly, the Yorkshire authorities were less than enamoured with the idea of a league in the county which was not under their control. Thirdly, there was the Reverend Frank Marshall the judge, jury and executioner with regard to professionalism within the game. To him a league was just one more step down the slippery slope to professional rugby and he was fervently opposed to the idea.

It appeared that the clubs considered discretion the better part of valour with regard to this initial plan and they set about modifying their original intentions. They were going to be quite conciliatory toward the Yorkshire Rugby Union authorities. They proposed to form an Alliance which would in no way oppose the authority of the county union. It was the Yorkshire Evening Post that published the news in its edition of 18th May 1892.[1]

**"At a private meeting held at the Saracen's Head Hotel, Leeds, last evening, the promoters of the new football organisation had the satisfaction of seeing their new scheme fairly set afloat. It should be stated at the outset that it was the evident and sincere wish of those connected with the matter that there should not be any conflict with the Yorkshire Rugby Union, and in proof of this we are informed that a resolution was adopted to the effect that any case where players**

---

[1] Yorkshire Evening Post May 18th 1892

**are selected to do duty for Yorkshire County or in the International matches, they shall do so irrespective of the fact that their clubs are engaged in championship matches in connection with the Alliance on that same date."**

The article went on to inform the reader of both the secret nature of the initial meetings along with the claim that those clubs who had suggested setting up a league had intended to obtain power either with or without the consent of the Yorkshire authorities. The new Alliance now stated they would need to get permission from the authorities. The softening of attitude from the clubs was quite marked as they now proposed that their intention was simply have an arrangement between certain clubs to play each other throughout the season. It was a proposal that other clubs of equal standing were opposed to, the likes of Manningham, Hull, Heckmondwike, Castleford, Holbeck, Pontefract and Leeds Parish Church. They claimed they were not prepared to stand idly by and allow those ten clubs to have the right to call their matches as 'Championship' games.

Following the meeting the Alliance Secretary, Mr Scarborough of the Halifax club told reporters that the scheme was to be laid before the Yorkshire Rugby Union at a special general meeting. It was obvious that the threat initially of a break away league within the county had been taken very seriously by the authorities and they were happy to now meet with the ten clubs. The question is just why did the clubs feel they needed to take this action and their answer was a simple one.

As they pointed out, at the time with the Yorkshire Cup competition scheme any success was dependent upon the draw. If a club was to lose in an early round, then all interest for the rest of the season was gone. With the proposed Alliance League supporters would have their interest maintained all through the season. That being the case the Alliance clubs would be assured of good gates all season long. To that end the senior clubs were going to press on with their efforts to form an Alliance.

Just a few days later the Alliance publicised a copy of the proposals they intended to place before the Yorkshire Rugby Union authorities. The York Herald on 23rd May published the same:-[2]

**"1. That this amalgamation of clubs be called the Yorkshire Football Alliance, and shall for the first season consist of the following ten clubs:- Bradford, Huddersfield, Halifax. Hunslet, Leeds, Liversedge, Dewsbury, Batley, Brighouse Rangers and Wakefield Trinity.**

**2. All matches shall be played under the rules of the Rugby Union and Yorkshire Rugby Union, and shall be of eighty minutes duration, unless otherwise mutually agreed upon.**

---

[2] York Herald 23 May 1892

3. All matches shall be arranged at an Alliance meeting specially convened for that purpose; at this meeting a date shall be fixed for concluding the competition which shall be before the first round of the Yorkshire Rugby Union Challenge Cup competition.

4. At the end of the competition the club scoring the largest number of points shall be declared the champion club of this Alliance, should two or more clubs be equal in points the club having the best score average (goals and tries) to be the winners. The scoring shall be two points for a win and one point for a draw.

5. The champion club to hold for the time being any trophy which may afterwards be decided upon.

6. A committee consisting of a representative from each of the competing clubs shall manage the competition.

7. That the secretary shall be a paid official, who shall not be allowed to vote at any meeting.

8. The two clubs having the lowest number of points shall retire compulsorily at the end of each competition, but shall be eligible for re-election. All elections shall be conducted by ballot. Application for membership of the Alliance to be made on or before March 1st."

While the proposals at first sight seemed to be quite innocuous it was the sixth one that initially would cause great concern for the authorities. That was simply because it involved them in giving up control of part of the game in the county to the ten clubs. This did not sit well with both members of the committee and also many of the other clubs not part of the Alliance. The second problem which would not present any difficulties until a few years later and that was proposal number eight. The fact that the bottom two clubs were to retire but would be eligible for re-election, in effect this meant the senior clubs could simply re-elect the bottom two clubs at the expense of any other club. Also, any club seeking a place in the Alliance needed to apply by the 1st March when the season was still ongoing.

That completed all that could be done now was to sit back and wait the special meeting of the Yorkshire authorities. At the same time, they were faced with dealing with the ever growing ill feeling generated towards the proposed Alliance by the rest of the clubs in the county. If that were not bad enough the Reverend Frank Marshall began a campaign intended to prevent the authorities granting the Alliance's wishes. He used the ever-present slippery road to professionalism as a reason for efforts to refuse the club's request.

If the ten clubs thought they were to be in for an easy ride in their quest they were sadly mistaken. The Yorkshire authorities convened a meeting on 13th June in Leeds to consider the proposals from the Alliance clubs. The Yorkshire Evening Post on that date carried the following article:[3]

"Great interest is taken in the annual meeting of the Yorkshire Rugby Football Union which is to be held this evening at the Queen's Hotel, Leeds. The chief cause is the uncertainty which appears to exist as to the course to be adopted by those who are interested in the promotion of the Yorkshire Football Alliance. A proposition is on the agenda paper to alter a bye-law so that it is not only necessary that such a combination should have the consent of the Union, but that it should be the first business after the election of officers at the annual meeting. If that is adopted it will, of course, be impossible to bring the matter forward this year at all. There are those who say that if anything in the way of stopping the formation of the Alliance is attempted some of the clubs will resign membership of the Union and stick to the Alliance. On the other hand, there are several clubs in the Alliance who have made it a *sine-qua-non* that there shall be no resistance to the authority of the Yorkshire Rugby Union."

It would seem that Marshall and his supporters were intent on using a technicality in the bye-laws to thwart the efforts of the ten clubs and were prepared as we shall see to go to any lengths to achieve their aim. While all of this was going on in Yorkshire across the Pennines the

---

[3] Yorkshire Evening Post 13 June 1892

senior clubs in Lancashire were eyeing the proceedings and making their own moves to ensure they were not left behind by their Yorkshire rivals. They however were not to face the same problems as did the white rose teams. It would not be unreasonable to make the assumption even after all this time that there would have been a dialogue between the senior clubs in Lancashire and those in Yorkshire. The topic of conversation undoubtedly would have been how to obtain greater autonomy from their respective county unions.

In Lancashire the Liverpool Mercury reported on a proposal by the Lancashire clubs to form themselves into a body in its issue on 3rd June 1892:- [4]

**"In Manchester last night a most important meeting of Lancashire rugby clubs was held to consider the advisability of forming a League. Salford, Swinton, Oldham, Wigan, Warrington, Liverpool, Liverpool Old Boys, Broughton and Broughton Rangers were represented Manchester having sent a letter upon the subject. It was expected that the Manchester and Liverpool clubs would offer objections to the scheme but the Liverpool ones gave their approval. Full arrangements will be made at a meeting to be held in Manchester on June 16th."**

It seemed the Lancashire authorities felt they were under no threat from the proposals made by the senior clubs and were happy to go along with the scheme to form a

---

[4] Liverpool Mercury 3 June 1892

league. No doubt they would have been aware of the situation over the Pennines and would not want to be left behind should an Alliance League eventuate. Equally important was that there seemed to be little opposition to the scheme from other clubs in Lancashire. It must be said that the number of clubs and their relative playing strength did not match that of Yorkshire. Yorkshire was without doubt the strongest rugby county in the country and had a far larger number of clubs under its auspices than any other county. The other thing to note is that the Lancashire clubs made no mention of wanting to control the league themselves they were happy to leave that in the hands of the authorities.

So it was that just two weeks later the Lancashire clubs met once more and the proceedings were again reported on by the Manchester Courier on 17th June:- [5]

**"An important meeting of secretaries of Lancashire rugby clubs was held at the Crown Hotel in Manchester last night, those present being Messrs Murray Swinton, Higson Salford, Warren Warrington, Wardle Wigan, Platt Oldham, Davies Broughton Rangers and Aitken Manchester. Mr Murray reported that Liverpool and Liverpool Old Boys could not see their way to join, and Mr. Aitken stated that his club could not entertain the idea this season on account of their fixtures being completed. It was a general expression of opinion that the league**

---

[5] Manchester Courier 17 June 1892

should start next season and it was resolved that it should be made up of; Swinton, Salford, Warrington, Wigan, Oldham, Broughton, Broughton Rangers and St. Helens Recs.

All these clubs with the exception of Salford and Wigan have home and home matches with each other, and it is the intention of the two clubs named to arrange fixtures to make the list of the League arrangements complete. Rochdale Hornets would have been included, but it was explained that they could not possibly arrange their fixtures so as to make them eligible, and for the next season at any rate they cannot enter. A sub committee was appointed to draw up rules, and Mr. Murray was appointed Hon Secretary."

There was very little sign of disagreement to these arrangement from the Reverend Marshall. It would appear his zeal and enthusiasm to stamp out professionalism did not extend outside the borders of the white rose county into 'enemy' territory. The truth be told the newspapers over in Yorkshire seem to be lauding the approach adopted by the Lancashire authorities while castigating that of the Yorkshire body. Certainly, that would seem the case from an article in the Leeds Times on 23rd June;-[6]

**"Whilst the Yorkshire Rugby Union are pretending to be so terribly frightened by the proposed football**

---

[6] Leeds Times 23 June 1892

alliance it is interesting to learn the attitude taken up by the Lancashire authorities. Have they foamed at the mouth and gone into hysterics? Not much. They are giving the scheme encouragement, and when it comes up for the sanction of the English Rugby Union they will not offer opposition to it. That at least is the current information. Is Yorkshire likely to get less than Lancashire in this matter? Hardly likely.

The ten can form themselves into a new West Riding Football Union; cease their membership with the Yorkshire Union; and I doubt not get the sanction of the English Rugby Union quite easily. They have plenty of ways of defeating the stupid juvenile opposition of the Yorkshire Union, and if they will only keep cool they can do so easily enough. I hope they will go straight on with their project now and teach the young bloods of the Yorkshire Union to be a bit more reasonable in future. But perhaps that is more than can be expected from the woolly-headed seventy.

It puzzles me rarely why the aforesaid Seventy should ever want to interfere with the Alliance. It cannot possibly affect them. They aren't left out in the cold, because it is a million to one against any of them being good enough even to be walked upon by the Alliance clubs. That is putting it strongly; but it is a fact that hardly any of them will ever get into the second-class, let alone the first-class ranks. One or two clubs may be aggrieved because they are not

**included in the ten. But they forget that everything must have a beginning, If, instead of childishly opposing the Alliance they had tried to co-operate and get a second and third sections of it formed, merit would soon have had a chance of getting to the top. Only a beginning must be made somewhere and it is obviously impossible to include the whole county in the first selection."**

The reporter was certainly not mincing his words nor could his opinion be misconstrued. He had identified one of the problems which would lead in the near future to an escalation in the dispute between the Alliance, the Union and the Reverend Marshall, namely the power wielded by the junior clubs who out numbered the senior clubs in the county. Equally importantly was the reporter's endorsement of the approach of the Lancashire Rugby Union with regard to league rugby. Not for the first time some in authority would continue to bury their head in the sand or hide behind the threat of the dreaded professionalism.

Over in Lancashire the authorities were taking a more pragmatic approach to the issue. One must wonder if they were in fact influenced by the approach adopted by the Football League where they were happy for amateurs and professionals to play together. There were quite a number of Association Football clubs in that county, six were in the first division and three in the second division and they all were attracting ever increasing crowds. That being the case the attitude seemed to be if their system works why not copy it providing you stay within the guidelines issued by the English Rugby Union. Also, The West Lancashire Union had introduced league rugby back in 1889 so such football was not new to the county.

Back in Yorkshire the Alliance awaited events at the AGM of the Yorkshire Rugby Union. Evidence suggests that both sides in the affair had a hidden agenda but officialdom had Frank Marshall and he held more sway. The York Herald carried an account of the AGM that showed just how far Marshall was prepared to go to ensure the Alliance was defeated in its edition of 18th June:-[7]

**"The Rev. F. Marshall rose to move the following alteration of bye-law 19;- 'After the word Union in line 4, to read At the Annual General Meeting, and the consideration of such rules shall be the first business, after the election of officers, of the meeting at which the said rules are submitted.'**

**Mr. George Harrop (Huddersfield) submitted that Mr. Marshall was out of order on the grounds that the proposed alteration had not been advertised according to rule.**

**The Chairman overruled the objection; and Mr Marshall proceeded to move his resolution, Which he pointed out was intended to secure the discussion of the proposed Yorkshire Football Alliance at the**

---

[7] York Herald 18 June 1892

annual general meeting of the Union only. He had heard one of the prominent supporters of the proposed Alliance observe that if the question of the Alliance could only be brought forward at a special meeting of the County Union the promotors would have a better chance of getting the scheme passed, inasmuch as the junior clubs would not be in attendance on the grounds of expense.

Mr. Harrop: Name!

Mr Marshall said he was prepared to give the name if desired.

The request for the name was repeated, and

Mr. Marshall: Mr. George Harrop is the gentleman.

Mr. Harrop:- I give it the lie direct. (sensation)

Mr. Marshall, taking no notice of Mr. Harrop's remark, said he had no argument to offer for or against the proposed Alliance, but he did seek to have the matter brought before all the clubs in the Union. The Alliance would either be beneficial or deleterious to Yorkshire football; and the scheme ought to be thoroughly ventilated. (Applause)

Mr. Miller seconded.

Mr. Harrop opposed the motion. He said that Mr. Marshall had been found out lying before and had lied that night (Loud cried of "Order" and "Chair".)

The Chairman called upon Mr. Harrop to withdraw the remark. (Applause)

Mr. Harrop: I withdraw it, having said it. (Cries of "Order".)

The Chairman: Without qualification.

Mr Harrop: I withdraw it, (Applause) Proceeding he said that the proposed Alliance would be constituted by ten of the principle clubs in Yorkshire; and he believed it would tend to the best interests of football in the county. Mr Marshall's motion would put back its formation for twelve months; and he (Mr. Harrop) thought this policy unwise.

Mr. Berry (Wakefield Trinity) and Mr. Haigh (Bradford) also opposed the resolution.

Mr. Marshall briefly replied, observing in regard to Mr. Harrop's imputation that he simply refuted the assertion, and if Mr. Harrop denied it. It would not hurt him. The only point the meeting had to consider was whether the question of an Alliance should be discussed at the annual general meeting or a special general meeting.

The resolution was then put and carried by 70 votes to 23."

The vote effectively meant that the Alliance could not move forward for at least twelve months and the next AGM. What Marshall succeeded in doing was to ensure the smaller clubs were able to be present to vote on so important a matter as the formation of an Alliance League. The Alliance were not exactly whiter than snow in the matter either. They desperately wanted the whole question discussed at a special meeting. The reason being that a great many of the smaller clubs would not be able to attend the meeting due to the cost of travelling to Leeds. Therefore, a smaller attendance gave the Alliance a better chance they thought of winning the day with their plans.

Following the meeting the Alliance clubs met to discuss the matter and the general feeling was that it was inadvisable that the whole issue was discussed by all of the clubs in the county. Sadness was expressed at the way in which the bye-law had been altered and the reason behind the change. However, at that meeting both the Dewsbury and Huddersfield clubs were not present as a result a resolution was passed that no definite decision as to further action be taken at that time. Feelings were mixed, some clubs were of the opinion they had not received fair treatment at the AGM others were of the opinion that they should accept the decision of the annual meeting.

There was a growing feeling in the county that the ten clubs had not been well treated and they were reluctant to wait a further year before forming the Alliance. As was pointed out there was no guarantee at an AGM that they would carry the day given all clubs big or small had an equal vote. One thing was certain, the issue was not over, even if the authorities thought that was the case. The Yorkshire Evening Post on 25th June reported on further developments after the clubs had met on the previous evening:-[8]

**"Present at the meeting were representatives of the Leeds, Huddersfield, Dewsbury, Batley, Brighouse Rangers, Liversedge, Halifax, Hunslet and Wakefield Trinity clubs.**

**A resolution was adopted condemning the unsportsmanlike manner in which the Yorkshire Rugby Union had at its annual meeting, shelved the Alliance question, nominally for twelve months, but practically for two years. It was felt that the promoters of the Alliance scheme had done everything in their power to prevent the combination from interfering in anyway with the Yorkshire Union, and that they had therefore merited fair treatment. A strong protest was entered against the action of the County Committee in reserving to themselves the right, in defiance of the bye-laws, of proposing alterations of, and additions to the agenda paper for the annual meeting."**

Feelings were running so high that in defiance of previous resolution to the contrary the clubs took the decision to continue in their quest to form an Alliance. Their next step was to effectively go over the head of the Yorkshire Rugby Union authorities and place their plans

---

[8] Yorkshire Evening Post 25 June 1892

before the English Rugby Union down in London. In doing so they resolved to explain the manner in which they had been treated by the county authorities at the annual meeting. More concerning was that the clubs made the decision that should the English Rugby Union throw the proposal back onto the Yorkshire authorities the Alliance would take matters into their own hands and **'form a Union among themselves, severing all connection with the existing Yorkshire Union.'**

It was a risky strategy by the clubs but they felt they had a strong case. They argued that the Yorkshire Rugby Union had no knowledge of their scheme a claim which was denied by the County Committee. The President of the Hunslet club, Mr. Wright told reporters that he had personally asked the Hunslet representative for such details and received a flat refusal. It was difficult to know just who was telling the truth at this point. The whole issue was getting very nasty with claim and counter claim coming from both sides. The problem for the clubs was a simple one, it was hard to see the authorities down in London deciding on a course of action contrary to that already agreed upon by the Yorkshire authorities. Still they persisted in their intention of appealing to the parent body.

All that could be done now by all parties was to sit back and await the upcoming meeting of the English Rugby Union in London. The waters were being somewhat muddied by another similar issue, as at that same meeting in London the senior clubs in Lancashire via their own County Committee were seeking approval for their proposal for league rugby in the county. The Lancashire authorities while in favour of setting up a league felt as a matter of curtesy, they should put their proposal to the parent body. The meeting was held at the Craven Hotel in London on 19th July and present were Mr. Scarborough from Halifax, Mr. Rhodes from Bradford, Alderman Riley from Halifax and Mr. Sewell from Leeds. There were no representatives present from Lancashire simply because they thought their request was going to be granted without discussion as it was not being opposed by the Lancashire authorities. The actual meeting was held in private. However the Yorkshire Evening Post on 20th July carried a report of what proceedings were known:- [9]

**"After a lengthy discussion extending over an hour took place. At the end of that time the deputation was again admitted to the room, and it was announced that the following resolution had been adopted:**

**'That this committee refuse to sanction the proposal before them to form an alliance in Yorkshire and a league in Lancashire.'**

**No one can be very much surprised with this result of the meeting inasmuch as the governing body have only by the resolution followed the traditions that have governed their action in the part, and firmly refused to sanction the formation of any organisation**

---
[9] Yorkshire Evening Post 20 July 1892

**not directly and thoroughly under the control of the committee to whom the Union has delegated the government of the game in their respective counties. What its effect on Yorkshire football will be is another matter, but at present it is impossible to say how the defeat will be accepted by the clubs concerned."**

It was a bitter blow to the Yorkshire clubs but even more so for the Lancashire clubs as they were not proposing to be independent of county control but it seems both proposals were tarred with the same brush by the authorities in London. All the decision did was store up resentment in clubs from both counties against the governing bodies. Back in Leeds the news was greeted with mixed feelings. Many held the opinion that the Alliance proposal contained nothing that the county authorities could take umbrage to. The Rugby Union however by previous decisions had shown they were not prepared to allow any body to menace the powers they had vested in themselves.

The reporter went on to speculate just what the next move could be by the senior clubs and concluded there were two options. Firstly, the Alliance proposals should be now dropped completely. Secondly, the clubs could secede from the Rugby Union completely and go it alone. The evidence he suggested was that when the clubs met in Leeds this is what it would actually do and form their own union. The down side to such action was that players turning out for clubs in the Alliance would have to give up any hope of gaining county or international honours. In addition, the ten clubs playing each other constantly would become monotonous.

It was then that the reporter made the point that would have sent a shiver down the spine of every county committeeman in both authorities:-

**"On the other hand, it must not be forgotten that the proposed League of Lancashire clubs, which had a similar veto put on it last night by the Rugby Union, may be an important factor in the situation. It had been thought that the Lancashire County Committee were willing to accept that organisation in the same manner that the Yorkshire Rugby Union were asked to receive the Yorkshire Alliance, namely, on the understanding that there should be no 'clashing' between the two bodies....**

**And the question which is now being asked by those who favour the Alliance is, 'Why should we not join with the Lancashire League and thus form a strong organisation, home and home matches between the component clubs, which would extend over the whole football season?' It is pointed out that by means of introducing clubs from the two counties of Lancashire and Yorkshire into the scheme, additional interest might be given to the matches."**

It was a proposal that seemed to generate a great deal of discussion in Yorkshire, in Lancashire the clubs had not got that far. They had no dispute with the authorities and the authorities had no problems with the clubs. The feeling was they had suffered at the hands of an ill thought out proposal by the Yorkshire clubs. The problem was that decisions had to be made by the Yorkshire outfits. The idea of a northern league was an idea that had been muted off and on for a number of years.

We got a better idea of just what had gone on at the meeting down in London from a report on 22nd July in the Yorkshire Evening Post. The ten clubs had met at the Old George Hotel in Briggate, Leeds. There the representatives who had travelled down to the meeting in London reported to the rest their thoughts and what information they had gleamed from the English Rugby Union. The reporter stated:-[10]

**"These gentlemen reported that they had been courteously received by the members of the English Union, but the opinion of that body was most emphatically that combinations of this nature must inevitably lead to professionalism, and that no such schemes could, on that ground alone, be sanctioned."**

There was a great deal of dissatisfaction from those present at the decision and a long discussion as to what should happen next took place. One suggestion was that the ten clubs as a body should withdraw from the Yorkshire Rugby Union but retain membership of the English Union. They would profess adherence to that

---
[10] Yorkshire Evening Post 22 July 1892

particular body and submit to its rules. The problem was that by leaving the Yorkshire Union it would inevitably mean they would also be leaving the English body. The decision was taken to leave the matter open and all would return to their respective clubs and consult with their club committees.

Such was the strength of feeling generated that all were of the opinion that their club committee would recommend resigning from both bodies. The view was also expressed that the opinions of the players were of equal importance for if the clubs were to leave the Rugby Union the players would forego any opportunity of obtaining county or international honours. There was yet another proposal discussed whereby it was felt that it may be possible to combine with the ten Lancashire clubs who were looking to form a League of their own.

At the meeting the Manningham club were represented by Mr. Jowett the Secretary and Mr. Holmes. They had attended to ascertain the scope and objects of the Alliance. Equally important they asked the question was there a possibility the group could be extended from the present ten clubs. It was a question many had considered and the view was that if twelve clubs were decided upon then Manningham should be one and a decision made between the likes of Hull, Castleford or some other club being approached to join the Alliance. There was one other interesting point raised at that meeting and reported on, namely, the setting up of 'District Unions'.

These had been created in 1891 and the senior clubs main grouse was a simple one, that instead of having power that corresponded to the importance of the club, power was invested equally into the hands of the smaller clubs in each district. It was a case as they saw it of the tail wagging the dog. More often as not a senior club could be outvoted by a number of smaller junior clubs on any matter brought to the District Union. All were of the opinion however, that leaving the Yorkshire Rugby Union would constitute a very serious step and was not to be taken lightly. Little did the clubs know at the time but such a proposal was perhaps their greatest weapon.

The Yorkshire County was without doubt the strongest in the country, of the county championships contested from 1887 to the time of the meeting in 1892 the championship had been won by the white rose on five occasions the only other winner was Lancashire. It was a situation the Yorkshire Committee held very dear and if the ten senior clubs were to secede then at a stroke the counties dominance could be wiped out. As will be seen it was a situation the authorities would do anything to avoid. What was also becoming clear was the growing ill feeling the smaller clubs had toward the ten senior clubs in the county, feeling they were not acting in the best interests of the game.

The members of the committee did return to their respective clubs and great discussions ensued. As was ever the case no one really wanted to make the ultimate decision and discussions between the two bodies the clubs and the authorities continued. The situation was to drag on until well into August and the new season was fast approaching. In Yorkshire it seemed that there was an endless round of meetings between the two bodies as well as meeting within the two bodies. Over in Lancashire there was total silence. The authorities there had sorted out the problem of the English Union refusing to sanction the proposed league. They took the decision that they themselves as an authority would institute a league system within the county for a number of senior clubs via their own bye-laws. Their bye-laws allowed them to establish any competition they saw fit.

In Yorkshire tensions continued running high, and as was the case back then all the drama was played out in the newspapers. On Friday 12th August The Yorkshire authorities held a meeting at which the question of the Alliance was discussed yet again. This meeting was called to discuss the events that had transpired between the two bodies at a joint meeting held a few days prior. The delegation from the authorities reported to the committee the events of that meeting. The outcome of that was an acceptance of the playing of a league was inevitable and to a large extent acceptable.

The sticking point was the one that had been present from the very first discussions, namely clause three of the Alliance's original proposals. This stated that the affairs of the Alliance be run by a committee consisting of one member from each of the ten clubs making up the Alliance. In truth this was a none starter as the English

Rugby Union had ruled against this insisting the Yorkshire Rugby Union were the sole official body controlling the game on behalf of the Union. The obvious solution was simply for the Yorkshire authorities to take on responsibility for running the Alliance League.

Strange as it may seem one of the reasons the authorities were reluctant to do that was the fear that as in cricket other clubs in the county would also like to be part of a league. The second reason was that other clubs of similar standing and strength as the ten making up the Alliance would raise objections to their matches being designated 'Championship' or 'Alliance' matches. The reporter revealed that one suggestion discussed at the meeting was:- [11]

**"There was also a suggestion made that by some arrangement the various organisations might be classed as 'first,' 'second', 'third', and succeeding numbers of competitions, a distinction being made between senior and junior clubs, and the two worst clubs in the first alliance should at the end of the first season exchange places with the two best of the second alliance team. This would be continued all through the grade and thus an opportunity would be given to the junior clubs to gradually force their way to the front."**

---

[11] Yorkshire Evening Post 12 August 1892

There was no doubt that the feeling was that a league system should be introduced with promotion and relegation as the 'norm'. As we shall see that idea was to become the root of all evil in just a few short years. The problem was that even as these suggestions were being discussed the Alliance made it very clear that they would not accept any system that did not give them a separate existence. They did state that they were willing to work under the control of the Yorkshire authorities but wanted to control the league themselves. It was a stance seemingly doomed to failure as we had seen, simply because it would not be sanctioned by the English Union. The straw the Alliance was clutching at was that throughout the county the cup competition was in the hands of a separate committee. What they failed to accept was that committee acted as a sub-committee of and under the control of the Yorkshire Rugby Union.

The following day 13th August the Yorkshire Evening Post reported on matters discussed at the meeting and there were one or two startling revelations. It was revealed that the sub-committee that had met with the ten clubs of the Alliance were recommending that a number of leagues should be set up. The problem was a simple one, because of the manipulation of the bye-laws by The Reverend Frank Marshall that action had forced the Alliance to take the only course of action they saw being open to them. Namely to appeal to the English Union, the decision of that Union had also caused some difficulties for the authorities. As a result, the Yorkshire authorities could not sanction any scheme that gave up control of the game from the county authorities.

As this was the major sticking point for the Alliance no progress seemed possible. Equally important to the clubs was the feeling that the actions of Frank Marshall which had been supported by the Yorkshire authorities had forced them to appeal to the English Rugby Union. The sad thing was that the sub-committee that had met with the clubs were agreed that a league structure was the best way forward. However, the clubs had muddied the waters once again as one of that sub-committee a Mr. Shaw pointed out:-

**"He thought they might come to some terms by which they would not have these ten clubs severing themselves from the county. He pointed out that it had been emphatically stated at the interview which took place that the clubs would resign."**

The clubs were holding a gun to the head of the authorities by suggesting their possible resignation. Shaw suggested that the league may well be controlled by a committee which consisted of equal members from each of the two bodies, the authorities and the clubs. What was clear was that from the point of view of the Yorkshire Rugby Union they wanted a resolution which was satisfactory to themselves and the ten clubs. Others made the point that should the clubs resign from the Yorkshire Rugby Union there was no guarantee that the English Rugby Union would allow them to remain members of the English body. The clubs however, felt that was not the case and the English body would allow them to continue operating under their auspices. Just where that view point originated from is unclear, equally unclear is why the clubs thought the authorities in London would support them.

Some in the meeting questioned if the ten clubs had the right to resign from the county without knowing if their committee was in agreement with that course of action. After all the discussions the following resolution was adopted:-

**"Seeing that the English Rugby Union have refused to sanction any League or Alliance being formed in Yorkshire during the coming season, this Committee cannot in the face of such decision fall in with the wishes of the ten clubs comprising the proposed Alliance. This Committee are, however, of the opinion that a series of competitions are desirable in which the whole of the clubs in membership with the Yorkshire Rugby Union can take part; this Committee proposes to formulate some scheme for the carrying out of such competition, and to get the sanction of the English Rugby Union as early as possible."**

The authorities seemed to be bending over backwards to accommodate the clubs the question was simple, would the clubs be prepared to compromise themselves? If they conceded control to the authorities the league would go ahead and peace would reign, sadly they would not. The reporter in what was a long article reveal a very strange piece of information regarding the working of the English Rugby Union in this matter writing:-

"**On the motion of Mr. Wright, seconded by Mr. France, it was resolved unanimously:- 'That the representatives from the Yorkshire Rugby Union on the Rugby Union Committee be requested to explain to the Yorkshire Committee what transpires at the meetings of the Rugby Union Committee.' This action was taken because the representatives of the Yorkshire Rugby Union on the Rugby Union had in accordance with a pledge of secrecy, refused to divulge what took place at the meeting in London when sanction to the Alliance scheme was refused. It was stated that the members of the Alliance Committee had learned through their representatives everything that took place. It was also argued that the members of the Committee had a right to know what took place in London.**"

One wondered just what the English body had or wanted to hide by swearing those attending meetings to secrecy! It was a policy that had been in place for many years. However, if the Alliance delegation had in fact revealed what was said at the meeting but the Yorkshire delegation had not was it any wonder so much distrust was being generated between the two bodies.

True to form the Alliance clubs following the meeting came to the conclusion that the authorities while saying a great deal had offered nothing acceptable to them. They were still adamant they wanted control of the Alliance League. The clubs met the following evening 13th August at the Old George Hotel in Briggate, Leeds. There was a long debate as to just what the authorities were actually offering which in truth was quite a great deal. As ever the stumbling block was that the clubs had not been given complete control of running the proposed league. The clubs seemed unwilling or unable to accept that by their actions in going to the English Rugby Union and losing their argument they had tied the Yorkshire authorities hands. The English body had refused to sanction the Alliance and as they overruled the county there was little that could be done. The other stumbling block it seemed was the insistence by the authorities that any league would not be implemented until the 1893-94 season twelve months hence.

As was ever the case a great deal of criticism of the authorities ensued along with claims that the clubs had no idea what had transpired at the meeting in London. The tide of ill feeling against the clubs was shifting and turning against the authorities. In the end the clubs drew up and all signed the following resolutions:- [12]

**"Resolved that the Alliance scheme be abandoned.**

---

[12] Yorkshire Evening Post 15 August 1892.

**Unanimously passed, that owing to the illegal attitude taken by the Yorkshire Rugby Union by preventing the senior clubs, and also their refusal to postpone the draw for the Yorkshire Challenge Cup Competition, as understood to be promised by the sub-committee delegated to meet us on August 8th with a view to coming to an amicable arrangement, we, on behalf of our respective clubs do hereby regretfully tender our resignation from the Yorkshire Rugby Union."**

The resignation of the ten clubs from the Yorkshire authorities came as a surprise to supporters in the county as the feeling was that events had not deteriorated to that extent. Many inside and outside the game felt that the resignations were simply a ploy to force the authorities to meet the demands of the clubs. Certainly, the cup draw had not been made at that time and would not be made until after the authorities had met yet again. Reporters speculated that only then would one of two paths be taken, namely accept the resignations of the clubs and carry out the cup draw. Or postpose the draw for a few days to allow the clubs time to reconsider their decision.

The Yorkshire Evening Post published in the same article the views of a good number of districts in the county and the majority it would seem favoured the action taken by the senior clubs. However, the opinion of some of the smaller clubs in the whole of the county were in favour of accepting the resignations. It was all getting very messy and quite unlike what was happening on the other side of the Pennines. There as the Lancashire Rugby Union itself had introduced a league system it all went a head without any hitch or protest. There was an added problem for the authorities when it was revealed that the Hull club had applied to join the now supposedly defunct Alliance and were happy also to offer their resignation from the Yorkshire Rugby Union.

Over the next few days people from both sides of the dispute aired their views in the local press. Both wanting to occupy the moral high ground on the issue. One figure sadly missing in the whole affair was The Reverend Frank Marshall. It was his action in altering the bye-law at the recent AGM that had sparked the problems that were now threatening to tear the game apart in the white rose county. It seems having created the mischief he had adopted the position of keeping his head down and his powder dry. There is little doubt that also over those next few days members of both parties would have had informal discussions in attempts to find a way forward.

Those talks were successful for on 18th August at the Green Dragon Hotel the ten clubs met once again. There they discussed yet another offer from the authorities to meet with them to try to reconcile the differences. In a sop to the clubs the authorities had postposed the cup draw to help facilitate a further meeting. Certainly, the attitude of the other clubs was mixed but the general opinion in Yorkshire was that the majority sided with the ten clubs on the matter. This had made the authorities adopt a much more conciliatory attitude to the proposals made by the clubs.

The other issue discussed by the clubs was their attitude regarding the Leeds club. The reporter for the Yorkshire Evening Post on 19th August outlined the position:- [13]

**"The Leeds Club's Committee, it will be remembered, decided to secede from the Alliance when it appeared probable that that body would carry their scheme forward, even in the face of opposition from the Yorkshire Rugby Union. The question now is whether or not the clubs who are in the competition shall play the matches which have already been arranged with that club for the next season. This conduct was described as 'temporising with the Alliance,' and though it was known that the action was not approved by the members of the Leeds club as a body, those present at the meeting were unanimous in saying that they must make an example of Leeds. The delegates felt that Leeds had deserted them in the most critical moment it was possible to choose, and that had one or two other powerful organisations adopted a similar attitude the whole scheme must inevitably have ended in disaster."**

Leeds had been a member of the original scheme by the Yorkshire clubs but when the scheme had been turned down by the authorities had changed their minds, or had they. The club had written to the Alliance stating they

---

[13] Yorkshire Evening Post 19August 1892

could not support any move that went against the authority of the Rugby Union. The Alliance clubs had taken that to be a letter of resignation however, Leeds claimed that was not the case. It seems then as now nothing is what it seems in rugby league. A great deal of discussion took place on the issue some feeling that if fixtures were to go ahead against Leeds they would have the benefit of playing senior clubs in the county. They would do so without having had to risk the troubles clubs in the Alliance now faced.

The reporter also informed the reader that Hull had in fact also now tendered their resignation from the Yorkshire Rugby Union. As a result, the rest of the clubs took the decision to include Hull in any proposed league. The meeting also decided that they would yet again meet the authorities in an attempt to find a way forward through their difficulties. As the meeting broke up one of the delegated told the reporter:-

**"If the committee of the allied clubs wished to take the step of adhering to their withdrawal from membership of the Yorkshire Rugby Union, they could command the adhesion of at least 40 of the principal clubs in the county, and could have two Alliances."**

If that were to be true and as was mentioned earlier the pride the authorities took in being the strongest county in the country such a comment would have carried a great deal of weight with them. Equally worrying was that if the reporter was correct in his assumptions, then a group of forty clubs leaving the Union would be more than capable of forming a very strong and attractive competition with or without any approval from the authorities.

Finally on Monday 22nd August the two sides met and thrashed out an agreement. Prior to that joint meeting the authorities held a meeting of their own at which Mr Miller the President of the Union read out a scheme he had drafted which was to be put to the ten rebel clubs. I suppose one mark of progress was that for the first time we are told the meeting had only one chairman, all the previous meetings had been chaired by one from each side!

Once again a great deal of talking from both sides took place, finally a settlement was reached upon which both the authorities and the clubs could agree on. The Yorkshire Evening Post on 23rd August reported on the meeting and printed a copy of the settlement:-[14]

**"1 That a competition be instituted to be called 'The Yorkshire Rugby Football Union Senior Competition'.**

**2 That the competition be under the authority of the Yorkshire Rugby Football Union, and be limited to clubs in membership with the Yorkshire Rugby Football Union.**

---

[14] Yorkshire Evening Post 23 August 1892

3 That the competition for the present season be managed by the ten clubs, with power to add to their number.

4 That the management be vested in a committee of one representative from each of the clubs in the competition, who shall act as a sub-committee of the Yorkshire Rugby Football Union and shall send a report of their proceedings to the Yorkshire Rugby Football Union Committee for confirmation.

5 All matches shall be played under the Rules of the Rugby Union and shall be of 80 minutes duration, unless otherwise mutually agreed upon.

6 The scoring shall be by points – two points for a win and one point for a draw.

7 The club scoring the greatest number of points shall be declared the champion club of the competition for the season.

8 In the event of two or more clubs being equal in points the club having the best average score of goals and tries may be declared the winner, or the committee may order another match or matches to be played.

9 That the champion club be the holder of any trophy which may be afterwards decided upon, and shall retain the same for such time as the committee shall hereafter decide.

10 That the competition be completed on or before the first Saturday in March.

11 The two clubs having the lowest number of points shall retire at the end of each competition, but shall be eligible for re-election.

The Yorkshire Rugby Football Union delegate to the committee of the competition the following powers:-

1 The decision of all questions of qualification.

2 The adjudication upon all questions of broken engagements and the fixing of dates for matches which cannot otherwise be mutually arranged.

3 The consideration of all protests, disputes, and complaints arising from the competition.

4 The decision of all questions of the championship.

5 The decision of all questions of transfer of players from clubs in the competition.

Whilst delegating these powers, the Yorkshire Rugby Football Union reserve to themselves the right at any time to adjudicate on any questions which may arise on an appeal being made to them, and shall have full power to alter or over-ride the decision of the sub-committee.

In case of appeal a deposit of £5 must be made, and the Yorkshire Rugby Football Union shall have

**absolute power to confiscate, return or otherwise deal with such deposit as they shall think fit.**

So it was that finally league rugby came into being in the county and the clubs were delighted seeing themselves as the victors in the dispute. That had won even more power than they had sought from the authorities a point acknowledged by the President James Miller. They say however, the devil is in the detail and so it was going to prove in the not-too-distant future. When clause number 3 is examined, it stated clearly that the clubs would have control over the new league but only for the first season. This fact would later be hotly disputed by the clubs.

If that were not problem enough going forward then clause number 11 was fraught with even more difficulties. This stated that the bottom two clubs would have to retire but would be eligible to be re-elected. At the time some expressed doubts about giving the club such powers feeling promotion should occur automatically. Clause number 4 was also somewhat confusing and would lead to problems in the future. It was that clause that had allowed the county authorities to give the new league the go ahead. They would argue that as the league committee had to submit its minutes for approval to the authorities the authorities were actually controlling the league. It was a document with a number of disputes waiting to happen in the near future. What the clubs also failed to recognise was the virtual power of veto over the whole competition the Yorkshire Rugby Union had given to themselves and that it had been agreed to by the clubs. It was this clause as was stated earlier that had allowed the county authorities to circumvent the need to go back to the authorities down in London.

It would be true to say that while a truce had finally been agreed it was at best an uneasy truce between the two competing bodies. Many in the authorities were less that happy that their authority had been usurped as they perceived and they were to have very long memories. A good many junior clubs were also less than happy with the outcome obtained by the senior clubs. Equally they were angry at the manner in which those privileges had been obtained, effectively they felt the club's resignations was in effect blackmail and they also were to have long memories. Many clubs on the other hand were happy with the outcome simply because they were to be part of the second, third or forth competition under the agreement. They actually believed that now a pathway had opened up for them to reach the very top level in the county, namely the Senior Competition.

The English Rugby Union while powerless to intervene were less than happy with the path the game seemed to be going down in the county. They were sure it was a path that would inevitably lead to professionalism in some form or another. Their fears were confirmed to a certain extend that trouble lay ahead as will be seen when later in the year the Yorkshire representatives James Miller and Mark Newcome at the AGM of the

Union proposed that clubs be allowed to pay bone fide broken time payments to players.

On the other side of the coin so to speak the ten clubs were also less than happy. They still saw the District Unions whereby a smaller area of the county was controlled by a sub-committee as problematic. The problem in their eyes was a simple one, each club in that district had an equal vote so a junior club had the same rights as one of the ten championship clubs. The clubs saw themselves being easily out voted on any issue they may well bring forward. Also, as time went on, they formed a loyalty to themselves as they were the founders of the championship that many saw as very inward looking, narrow and even parochial. It was this that was eventually to prove to be their undoing.

For now, they set about enjoying their new found freedom and the approach they were adopting was made very clear in the very first sub-committee meeting they held. They held their first meeting on 30th August at the Talbot Hotel in Bradford and the first order of business was to identify the ten members, one from each club who would form the sub-committee controlling the championship. The report of that meeting clearly shows the mind set of the ten clubs and just how they intended to go about running the newly formed league.

The York Herald on August 31st carried a report of the meeting and two issues raised show the way the senior clubs were going to go with their thinking. Firstly:- [15]

"The first business was the consideration of applications to join the allied clubs from Kirkstall, Castleford and Heckmondwike and a deputation from the last named club also waited upon the committee. A resolution was come to expressing the opinion of the committee that the scheme at present was already large enough, and that though the names of the clubs mentioned would receive favourable consideration at the end of the season, at present the competition could not be enlarged."

We know that come the end of the season it was Hull and Leeds that were elected to increase the league from ten to twelve clubs. The second piece of business brought to the fore the hoary problem of promotion and relegation into the senior competition that was not going to go away:-

"An application was also received from Mr Johnson, of Wortley, on behalf of the second combination in Yorkshire, asking the committee to receive a deputation with the view of the formation of another competition for clubs not included in the senior ten, and asking that the two highest Second Combination should be admitted each year to the senior ranks in the place of the lowest clubs in the Senior Competition. The committee decided that at present the proposition was premature, but they expressed a

---

[15] York Herald 31 August 1892

**willingness to meet a deputation from the second combination later in the season."**

As we now know the whole issue of promotion and relegation would eventually have a tremendous effect on the senior competition. Sadly, the writing was on the wall regarding promotion or the lack of it, very early in the life of the senior competition in Yorkshire and also over in Lancashire.

So it was that league rugby arrived in both Yorkshire and Lancashire and it has to be said it proved to be a tremendous success. There is no doubt that by Yorkshire introducing effectively a first, second, third and fourth division it eased many of the resentments junior clubs had against the senior outfits. Now clubs felt they could reach the very top level of the game in the county. The same situation occurred in Lancashire but it was a little more fair with regard to promotion, in that county simply because all three divisions were under the direct control of the county authorities.

The players were delighted by the introduction of a league system as now they saw games as having some meaning as they were playing for two points. Supporters were also delighted as they also now saw games as having some purpose. The clubs obviously were more than delighted as the fans came streaming back through the turn stiles thus filling the club's coffers once again. There was though trouble brewing on the horizon and a number of fronts.

*Rugby League is Born*

## CHAPTER TWO

### (1893)

As that first season had progressed the leagues in the two counties had flourished. The competition had been greatly welcomed by supporters and large crowds turned out to watch games. In Lancashire as the league season was coming to a close, supporters were still engaged as they looked for the promotion and relegation outcomes. As the leagues were under the control of the authorities such matters happened as a matter of course. The bottom club in the first division was ordered to play a 'Test' match against the winners of the second division. The winner would play the following season in the higher division.

In the white rose county league rugby was also proving a great success. On the field nothing really changed, the county won the County Championship defeating Cumberland. Domestically Bradford was crowned champions of the Senior Competition while Dewsbury and Wakefield Trinity occupied the bottom two places in the competition. In the second competition Holbeck had claimed the honours with Elland in runner up spot it was then problems emerged.

When the season came to an end the winners and runner up of the second competition expected to be promoted to the senior competition. Sadly, that did not happen and that created something of a stir in the county. The senior clubs at their meeting at the end of the season ordered

Dewsbury and Wakefield to retire from the competition. Both clubs were then asked to make a presentation to the committee as to why they should be re-elected. This the clubs did and they were retained in the senior competition. Obviously Holbeck and Elland were less than enamoured with the decision as was the committee running the Second Competition. They were of the opinion that their two clubs would and should replace Dewsbury and Wakefield. The outcry from other clubs in the county was equally loud but to no effect. The senior clubs did alleviate some of the rancour and outcry by expanding the senior division from ten to twelve. They did so by electing to bring in both Hull and Leeds. These were two long standing senior clubs and few could argue that they should be in the Senior Competition.

If the senior clubs felt that the matter was now at an end however, they were sadly mistaken for their action simply opened up old wounds and old grievances were revisited by junior clubs. A movement was growing ever stronger in the county that what was needed was a system of promotion on merit. Such a system was in place over the Pennines and was causing no problems why then could the same not be achieved in Yorkshire. In truth many clubs felt that such a system was already in place but its implementation was being thwarted by the actions of the senior clubs.

Those feelings were only partly right with regard to Lancashire. The problem of promotion and relegation was just as prevalent there but it took a different form in that county. It was an open secret within the game that clubs in the north of the country in general and in Lancashire and Yorkshire in particular were guilty of making illegal payments to players. These so-called broken time payments had been paid by clubs for years even though they were illegal. If a player needed to finish work early in order to be able to play for the club his lost wages were made up by the club.

In Lancashire there was a growing concern that clubs under the new league system were going beyond such payments. Rumours were rife that clubs were actually paying players to play on a match-by-match basis. Also, clubs were inducing players to leave their present club to play for them and by doing so were placed in more lucrative employment usually by a wealthy member of the new club. These actions by clubs was done in an attempt to either secure a promotion to a higher division or prevent relegation to a lower one.

In an effort to address the growing issue of broken time payments to players it would be the Yorkshire authorities that were to be prepared to raise and tackle matters. James Miller the President of the Yorkshire Union was proposing to take a motion to the upcoming AGM of the Rugby Union to be held on 20th September. His proposal was to be seconded by Mark Newsome from the Dewsbury club, its aim was to get the authorities to sanction such payments to players. It was a practice wide spread in the north albeit under the table. It was also prevalent in other parts of the country so the hope was that the resolution would be accepted at the AGM.

The proposal that Miller had drawn up read:-

**"That players be allowed compensation for bone-fide loss of time."**

It seemed a simple enough proposal but it generated a great deal of heat not only in Yorkshire but throughout the whole of the country.

The Yorkshire authorities in all probability had consultations with their counterpart in Lancashire and outlined their proposal. In truth they were preaching to the converted or so it would seem. Although not all the Lancashire clubs were in agreement for the Huddersfield Chronicle reported on a meeting at which correspondence from Lancashire was read out:- [16]

**"A letter was read by Mr Hirst (Hon Sec) from Mr J. H. Payne Hon Sec of the Lancashire County Committee conveying the resolution arrived at by the Lancashire representatives with regard to payment for broken time. Mr Payne stated that while opinion was fairly divided there was a majority in favour of the proposal of Mr Miller, and, accordingly, representatives of the Lancashire clubs would have a free hand."**

---

[16] Huddersfield Chronicle 20 September 1893

That would seem to suggest that clubs at the AGM in London would be free to vote as they wished. However, on that same day the Yorkshire Evening Post published an interesting snippet[17] in which it claimed to have evidence that a good number of minor Yorkshire clubs intended to oppose the motion. It would be claimed later that the motion was defeated via a good number of proxy votes that were of a somewhat dubious nature. Perhaps many were from those dissolute junior Yorkshire outfits.

The AGM was held on 20th September and a very detailed account was published by the Manchester Courier the following day [18]

The Yorkshire President Miller put forward his proposition and quite interestingly stated that it is in part due to action taken a few years earlier by the Rugby Union:-

**"Why was this proposition brought forward? Simply because of the change of conditions under which football is now played compared with years ago. It would be well to remember that the change had been brought about by the Union itself in order to popularise the game. But the Union in popularising the game had brought into the field a type of player vastly different to that of years gone by. In fact, players were no longer confined to the universities,**

---

[17] Yorkshire Evening Post 20 September
[18] Manchester Courier 21 September 1893

**public schools and the more favoured classes of the people. The Union had urged the game upon the people of the country, and the young working man in particular. More particularly had this been so in the great manufacturing centres of the north. The Union had recognised this change so far as it affected the game, but not in regard to the player. In the north that class of player was treated in a different manner to what they would have treated him years ago. It had not been realised in the south what difficulties the north had to contend with."**

It was a clever argument Miller used and he went on to state the injustice of a player having to lose wages in order to play the game. What he claimed rang true with some at the meeting the authorities were responsible for popularising the game. The problem that had been produced was only evident in the north where the game had attracted far more working class people. This was a phenomenon new to the authorities and they were at a loss as to how to tackle it in Miller's opinion. Other speakers who opposed the resolution argued that broken time was simply professionalism and that was an end to the matter it was not allowed as the laws stood. There were two other interesting points raised that evening the first coming from Newsome who felt that professionalism within the sport was inevitable. He believed that by sanctioning broken time the Rugby Union would be delaying the onset of such professionalism. He even went on to state that professionalism was but three years away, how right would he be proved to be.

The other argument put forward against the motion by the likes of the Union President William Cail was also a simple one. It was that Miller had not proposed a scheme whereby broken time payments could be managed, controlled, recorded and approved by the authorities. How could such a scheme work and what would happen to the minor clubs who could not afford to make such payments. Cail argued such clubs would go to the wall. The debate which was at time fiery and personal, particularly toward the Reverend Frank Marshall went on long into the night. Eventually when the vote was taken as we know in part due to some very dubious proxy votes, Miller's resolution was defeated by 136 to 282.

Sadly, the growing demand for broken time payments to be allowed was ever stronger rather than abating following the meeting. In Lancashire the clubs were taking the issue even further as rumours abounded that clubs were paying much more that broken time to their players. Many clubs found employment for players in order to attract then to the club. Some it was alleged were actually paying their players a wage for playing for the club. It was all getting very acrimonious particularly in Lancashire. In Yorkshire there were other issued related to promotion and relegation into the Senior

Competition to occupy the minds of club and county officials.

Problems for the Yorkshire clubs in general and the Huddersfield club in particular were increasing as the season was progressing. A charge of professionalism against the Huddersfield club was made by the Cumberland Rugby Union. It was alleged that a Huddersfield club official a Mr Hardy had been up to Cumberland to Cummersdale and there approached two of the Cummersdale Hornets players Boak and Forsythe. The upshot of his approach was that the two players who were at the time employed in the printing works in the village left Cummersdale and moved to Huddersfield. Once there they began playing for the Yorkshire outfit.

The claim made was that the players had been poached on the promise that they would receive thirty shillings per week while in Huddersfield. In addition, both players were found employment in the town. When the club actually selected the two players the committeeman none other than the Reverend Frank Marshall resigned from the committee. A meeting was held in Preston, Lancashire to investigate the claims on 13th October and the panel investigating was William Cail President of the Rugby Union who co-incidentally was also President of the Cumberland Rugby Union. Mr Curry the Vice-President of the Rugby Union and Mr. Crook from the Lancashire Rugby Union.

The actual meeting was held in secret and a good number of people including the two players and club officials were questioned. The clubs' defence had been that Hardy was a former member of the Huddersfield Committee but had resigned almost a year earlier and moved to Sheffield. After a lengthy hearing and a very short discussion the decision was that the two players were to be suspended. As for the Huddersfield club no decision was reached and it was decided to refer the matter to the authorities in London.

That meeting was held on 14th November in London and in keeping with the procedures of the day all those attending were sworn to secrecy before they were allowed to enter the meeting and give their evidence. The Huddersfield Chronicle reported on the outcome of the meeting.[19] They published the brief facts:-

**"Club suspended until the end of 1893. The meaning of this is plain. The club and none of its members can take part in any football match under Rugby Union rules until the expiration of the terms of suspension."**

The club and the Yorkshire authorities to a large extent were less than happy. The club felt that their evidence had not really been examined and given the consideration it deserved. There was also the feeling that as the original allegation had come from the Cumberland Rugby Union then its President William Cail should not

---

[19] Huddersfield Chronicle 15 November 1893

have been allowed to preside at the original meeting or in Preston on 13th October. It was all yet again very messy but the end result was the Yorkshire club was faced with serving a six week suspension. A good deal of resentment resulted from the whole episode.

*(Not a great deal is known of John Forsythe on the other hand a great deal is known of George Boak. This is due in the main to the work of the Huddersfield Rugby League Heritage who have videoed relatives of Boak. They have been able to fill out details of those events. A fuller account of Boak is available in the appendix at the end of the book.)*

## CHAPTER THREE

### (1894)

During this second season of league rugby in the two counties life went on as normal or as normal as rugby could ever be. The furore the Senior Competition had caused by not allowing promotion from the second competition at the end of the first season of league rugby had subsided but not gone away. It was once again to come to the forefront as the season came to a close. Brighouse and Manningham had ended the season on top of the table with 33 points each. The Senior Competition Committee ordered a play off between the two which failed to produce a winner and so a second replay was ordered. In the end Manningham prevailed winning the second play off 17-2.

True to form the county championship had again been won by Yorkshire and all seemed well with the world. The problem was that in the second competition Leeds Parish Church had been crowned champions and Holbeck runners up. Both clubs expected to be promoted into the senior competition as of right or on merit. That did not happen as that second season ended the senior clubs elected to retain the bottom two clubs Batley and Dewsbury. As was to be expected an out cry ensued and the authorities were less than pleased.

The senior clubs for their part did as they always did in such situations, nothing. The Yorkshire Committee however, were insistent that action needed to be taken by the senior clubs in this matter. Inevitably a meeting of the senior clubs was called at the Green Dragon Hotel, in Leeds. The Yorkshire Evening Post wrote an account of the senior clubs meeting in its issue of 13th April 1894:- [20]

**"An important meeting of the Sub-Committee of the Yorkshire Senior Competition was held last night at the Green Dragon Hotel, Leeds, to decide the constitution for the next season. According to the existing rules, the two lowest clubs in the competition must retire yearly, but are eligible for re-election. The two clubs concerned are Batley and Dewsbury. A deputation from the No. 2 Competition Committee asked that the two highest clubs in their competition should be admitted into the senior ranks. Applications were also made by Heckmondwike and Castleford. The committee, in considering the whole matter, first voted upon the question as to whether the competition next season should be increased to fourteen clubs or remain at twelve as at present, and it was ultimately decided that the number should remain at twelve. It was then unanimously resolved to alter Rule 28 as follows:-**

**That next season the bottom club in the Senior Competition shall retire and play the winner of the**

---

[20] Yorkshire Evening Post 13th April 1894

**Competition No.2 a deciding match, the winning club in such match to be included in the Senior Competition for the season following."**

Once again, the senior clubs attempted to play down the controversy following their decision not to admit the two second competition clubs Leeds Parish Church and Holbeck. The carrot they were dangling before the authorities was that the winner of the second division would be able to get into the senior competition if they defeated the bottom club in that competition. As will be seen it was simply a ruse to calm or attempt to calm the outrage they were creating with regard to promotion to the Senior Competition. They were determined to continue this ploy in order to preserve their self-preservation whatever the cost and ultimately that determination would lead to problems and their down fall.

Over in Lancashire they were having no such problems as promotion and relegation happened automatically. Sadly, the senior clubs there were having problems of a much more serious nature and they were problems that were attracting the attention of both the Lancashire and English Rugby Union. Those problems were being caused by professionalism or more accurately claims of professionalism. In their desire to secure promotion to a higher division clubs were offering inducements to players to leave their present club to join them. This was strictly against the new rules on professionalism introduced following the efforts of William Cail in 1893.

Not only that but rumours were circulating that clubs were actually paying wages to their players and it was this that was causing the greatest concern. The hard won freedoms clubs in both counties had acquired were coming under attack on a number of fronts and would sadly reach some sort of crisis point in 1894.

The evidence for the birth of the game of Northern Rugby Union suggests its origins initially lay in Lancashire. The problems in that county were to escalate and spread into Yorkshire where the Yorkshire clubs were determined to hang onto their freedoms whatever the cost. As was stated earlier the problems in the red rose county arose from the growth of professionalism within the game. All clubs knew they were able to reach the first division on merit and so were enticing players to leave a club and play for them. Or they would try to get players to come to the club to help them avoid relegation. In many cased financial inducements were being made to the players.

The most common method used was to offer to find a player a job should he join them. The other incentive was the age old 'broken time payment', when a player had to leave work early to play for the club, he lost wages. The club simply made up the wages he had lost but they were becoming ever more generous in the payment they made to a player. Gone was the old six shilling per day payment sums of thirty shilling seemed to be coming the norm rather than the exception. The crisis, for that was what it was, reached a serious level early in the 1894-95 season and it was the senior Lancashire clubs that were the catalyst.

There was a growing belief that all of the senior clubs in Lancashire were making payments to players. The Leigh club were investigated for offences of professionalism committed during the 1893-94 season. The Leeds Mercury[21] reported that on Wednesday 19th September the Lancashire Rugby Union met to discuss the allegations against the club. As was to be expected there was a large attendance including representatives from a great many senior clubs. Following a long discussion held in private Mr. Grover the Chairman called in the representatives from the Leigh club along with the reporters present to deliver the verdict:-

**"That certain offences against the law relating to professionalism have been committed by the Leigh Club, and the committee suspend them until the end of November."**

The charges were brought against the club by a Mr Battersby who claimed he was owed money by the club. He claimed that he had provided board and lodgings for two players who had travelled up from Wales to play for Leigh. Such action was prohibited by the rules on professionalism. It seems he was believed, and the club was not, by the authorities. The result was a ten week suspension of the Leigh club.

---

[21] Leeds Mercury 19th September 1894

It was a decision that affected not only the Leigh club but also all of the players who represented the club during the previous season when the offences were alleged to have occurred. It also sucked both Salford and Bradford into the controversy as the Leigh player Ewan had moved to the Salford club and Wilding had moved to Bradford. Both players found themselves suspended for ten weeks much to the annoyance of their new clubs. The other clubs in the first division were also affected as they needed to make a decision as to what to do about the league fixtures against Leigh while they were suspended. Sadly, Leigh were not the only ones accused of professionalism as it was becoming common knowledge that Salford were to answer similar charges.

The Gloucester Citizen in an article on 9th October when reporting on a case of a player from that county allegedly being poached by a Yorkshire club revealed a far more serious issue:-[22]

**"Before Leigh were suspended the 10 clubs in the Lancashire Rugby Competition were sounded about adopting professionalism, but thought the time was not yet ripe. Salford will now implicate three other clubs, and Leigh follow suit, and veiled professionalism in Lancashire and Yorkshire will then be displaced by open professionalism."**

On 16th October the Lancashire authorities gathered yet again this time to judge Salford. The club who admitted

---
[22] Gloucester Citizen 9th October 1894

the charges against them was found guilty of paying a player by the name of Joe Smith and as a result were suspended until the end of 1894.

*(Interestingly while Smith was branded a professional, he seems to have still wanted to play the game. When the Northern Union was formed in August 1895 he decided to apply to be reinstated as a Northern Union player. The Manchester Courier on 11th September 1895 reported that Smith had appeared before the sub-committee. His application was refused as the committee were 'against out and out professionalism'. In truth there was no other decision they could make after all they has been preaching to the newspapers since the split that the new league was opposed to professionalism in any form.)*

On the verdict being announced Mr. Higson the Secretary of the Salford club went onto the attack and stated he intended to lodge claims of professionalism against Swinton, Tyldesley, Rochdale Hornets, Broughton Rangers and Wigan. Also, while not directly accusing Oldham he did say the club was very clever in managing the manner in which it brought players to the club. Higson claimed that the Oldham club had acquired the services of Yorkshire County players and Welsh Internationals and wondered just how they had managed to persuade such players to the club.

There was little doubt that the senior Lancashire clubs were growing increasingly angry with the Lancashire authorities with regard to their attitude regarding them paying players. The authorities claimed their hands were tied by the new rules on professionalism introduced by the English Rugby Union. However, some on the Lancashire Committee were of the opinion that professionalism in a manner similar to that of the Football Association was the best way forward for the sport. The problem was that the Yorkshire clubs who had been dealing with their own problems with the authorities were being dragged into the professionalism debate.

The renowned rugby writer 'OLD EBOR' wrote a piece in the Yorkshire Evening Post following the Salford hearing on 17th October.[23] In it he examined the implications of that hearing with regard to the future of the game in both counties. He was full of praise for the Salford club for coming clean on what they had done and confessed their guilt. He was also happy to see that both sides of the Lancashire Committee those for and those against profesionalism being civil to each other. There was no doubt in his mind that some members of the committee were vehemently opposed to any form of professionalism while others felt such a path was inevitable.

He was a little more critical of the committee for not digging deeper into the matter writing:-

---

[23] Yorkshire Evening Post 17th October 1894

> "This brings me to a point at which it is necessary to point out that the Lancashire Committee were not quite as eager as they might have been to get to the bottom of the veiled professional business. Mr. Page, the Salford assistant secretary, said he paid Smith the money. Where did it come from? How was it entered in the books? On these points not a question was asked."

He posed the question were the committee not wanting to stir up any more mud than they had to in their investigations. He was also of the opinion that the punishment meted out was lenient being just ten weeks the same as that inflicted upon Leigh. As he wrote, now clubs will feel that if they are caught out breaking the professional rules, they will suffer only a ten week suspension. It was then he revealed to readers the bombshell that was exploded on the meeting or should that be after the meeting mentioned earlier :-

> "Mr. Higson informed me that the clubs whom Salford now charge with professionalism are the following:- Swinton, Tyldesley, Rochdale Hornets, Broughton Rangers and Wigan, adding sarcastically that a club which could manage to import Welsh internationals and Yorkshire County men must, of course, be above suspicion – this, it is obvious being a side hit at the Oldham club, whose officials have a reputation for more than average cleverness where football arrangements are concerned."

The Lancashire authorities stated they intended to investigate those claims. The question was, could they be proved. Certainly, the Lancashire first division was now thrown into chaos as two of their members were under suspension while five others were to be investigated. There was little doubt the other three clubs would also come under scrutiny which would put the whole of the first division under threat of suspension. With regard to the situation in both Lancashire and Yorkshire OLD EBOR was under no doubt where the future of rugby lay:-

**"So far as it is possible to form a judgement upon the condition of things in Lancashire and Yorkshire, I feel compelled to say that the time is at hand when clubs will have to choose whether they will play as amateurs or openly avow themselves as professionals. Amateurism pure and simple is in a distinct minority in both counties, That, is a bold statement to make, but it would be hypocritical to contend that it is not so, and I don't intend to do it. In some form or another professionalism has permeated the whole system of Rugby football in Lancashire and Yorkshire, and in justice to those counties it should be said there is good reason for thinking that the elements of misdoing, are not confined to their clubs nor to the north alone."**

What OLD EBOR was saying was that most of the clubs in the north and importantly in other parts of the country were actually breaking the professional laws laid down by the Rugby Union by paying broken time. The question again was a simple one, would the clubs in Lancashire and Yorkshire be forced down the road of open professionalism should the authorities adopt a firmer hand. On 18th October the Leeds Mercury informed the reader that the claims Mr Higson was making concerned individual players rather than general allegations.[24]

However, they also gave an insight into the differing attituded toward professionalism in the two counties. They reported a quote from the Yorkshire side of things:-

**"Charles Holdsworth Secretary of the Senior Competition is of the opinion that professionalism is inevitable in Lancashire but not in Yorkshire at present."**

What this statement tells us is that the issue of professionalism was something more pertinent to the red rose county than the white rose clubs. In fairness in Yorkshire the authorities seemed quite content to let their counterparts over the Pennines fight the professionalism battle they had their own battle to fight with the senior clubs.

They were involved in a dispute with the Alliance clubs who had control of the first division. The two parties had held a meeting on 11th October at the Green Dragon

---

[24] Leeds Mercury 18th October 1894

Hotel in Leeds under discussion was the promotion rule. As had always been the case since way back in 1892 the dispute focussed on the wordage of the rules. The Yorkshire Evening Post on 12th October had reported on the meeting writing :-[25]

**"The rule in dispute is number 28, which states, as now drafted by the Competition Committee, that the last club on the list shall retire, but be eligible for re-election, or it may be required to play a match with a club in the Second Competition. It is to the words, 'eligible for re-election' that the majority on the Yorkshire Union Committee take exception, and on which the controversy has arisen."**

It was obvious the County authorities wanted there to be promotion and relegation into the first division albeit via a 'Test' match if necessary. The clubs for their part were not prepared to give up their control on this issue and the excuse they put forward was controversial at best and downright bizarre at worst. Their objections to rewording bye-law 28 was:-

**"That they considered it absolutely necessary they should have some direct power of protecting clubs which through circumstances other than bad football, might be at the bottom of the list. It was pointed out that an epidemic, an accident to a number of players, or some other unforeseen circumstances might occur, as the result of which a club which had spent**

---

[25] Yorkshire Evening Post 12th October

**thousands of pounds and done a great work for football might be placed temporarily at the bottom of the list, and they considered it would be unwise and unfair to make that club run the risk of ruin as a first class organisation."**

Whichever way you look at that statement it was clear that the clubs that formed the first division were intent on ensuring the twelve of them were never to be relegated. It was a stand that was causing the rest of the clubs in Yorkshire that had stood firmly behind them back in 1892 to reverse their feelings. Various suggestions were put forward by the Yorkshire authorities as to altering the wording of bye-law number 28 all of which were rejected out of hand by the clubs. The clubs continued to say it was their intention to adhere to the bye-law wherever possible as a means of promotion via a 'Test' match. It was a statement few actually gave any credence to. After all the clubs had been successfully avoiding the issue for two years now and were seen by many as doing the same once again.

Following that meeting the Yorkshire authorities held a meeting at which it was resolved to propose altering the wording of bye-law number 28 and it would be brought before the full Yorkshire Rugby Union Committee at its next meeting. For their part the twelve clubs also held a meeting at which it unanimously approved the stance taken by their representatives. It was a case of an unstoppable force meeting an immovable object and it spelled trouble ahead. The reporter however, put a different slant on the growing conflict suggesting the dispute was not really between the Yorkshire authorities and the senior clubs. According to the reporter the senior clubs saw it as a dispute between themselves and the clubs in the second division and below, writing:-

**"While claiming to be as loyal to the county's best interests as anybody can be, the senior clubs are determined once and for all to show that in matters which concern their own interests they will not be ruled by the clubs below them."**

There was little doubt the senior clubs were seeking to gain the high moral ground in this dispute but as was stated earlier they were badly misreading the mood of the game throughout the county. Either that or they knew full well the feelings of the rest of the county but were not in the least bothered. They showed their disregard for the authorities and the clubs below them by a claim made to the reporter:-

**"In the event of the Yorkshire Union on Wednesday evening next again declining to sanction the rule, in all probability the Senior Competition Committee will take no further action in the matter, but proceed with their business as if nothing had happened. When the time comes for promoting one of the second-class clubs they will act as they consider the circumstances demand, and the battle will then commence in earnest."**

This dispute was raging in October 1894 not as is often claimed August, 1985, that was a dispute bound to happen. Way back in 1892 the English Rugby Union had stated quite clearly that they would not sanction any other body to control the game in Yorkshire other than the recognised authority. There was no doubt the senior clubs were facing a battle they could not win. So, in Yorkshire the dispute was over the issue of promotion and relegation. In Lancashire there was an equally serious dispute between the senior clubs and the authorities but that was over the issue of professionalism.

It is worthwhile making the point here that in both counties the disputes had nothing whatsoever to do with broken time payments to players. As we know come the great schism this was claimed to be the major issue between the clubs and the authorities in both counties. Evidence suggests that nothing could be further from the truth. While the Yorkshire senior clubs adopted a head in the sand approach and carried on as before there was no such action over the Pennines. There clubs were beginning to be proactive as they felt they at least had some sympathy for their problems from some senior members of the Lancashire Rugby Union Committee.

Down in London the Rugby Union was becoming increasingly concerned about the growing crisis in Lancashire with regard to professionalism. So worried were they that they had discussions with some members of the Lancashire authorities and it was agreed to hold a meeting to discuss the whole issue. That meeting was held at the Craven Hotel in London on 1st November. After a long debate the Union issued a circular and a copy of that circular to the press. It was to say the least quite draconian in its content as printed in the Birmingham Daily Post stating:-[26]

"Resolved:-

**1. That a circular be at once issued by this committee to the clubs of this union asking them whether they will undertake to comply with the letter and spirit of the bye-laws, rules and regulations of this union as regards professionalism and requesting a reply within twenty eight days from the date of the circular.**

**2. That offences committed by clubs after the issue of the circular, whether through themselves, their agents, officials, members or ticket holders, shall be punished by expulsion of such clubs and permanent suspension of all members and officials.**

**3. That the committee will consider applications for reinstatement on part of any members.**

**4. That having regard for the notorious methods of concealment hitherto adopted by offending clubs the committee will, in dealing with future cases, consider**

---

[26] Birmingham Daily Post 2nd November 1894

**the burden of proof of innocence lies on the club or person charged.**

**5. The committee will not suspend, or otherwise punish witnesses who voluntarily give evidence bona-fide to the union.**

**6. That when a player applies for his transfer the burden of proof of the bona-fide of his application shall lie on such player."**

It was an outrageous document in as much as it went against normal justice. The Union authorities were simply stating they did not need to prove guilt but rather the club or player needed to prove their innocence. When clubs in the north received the circular, they were outraged and it was not just those clubs in the north. Such was the clamour within the game that the Rugby Union was forced hastily to withdraw the offending circular. What the circular did show was the state of unease the Rugby Union was experiencing with regard to the growing trend of professionalism. Rather than adopt the approach of the rival code of Association Football and accept players could be amateur or professional they seemed determined to rid the game of all aspects of professionalism. Their mantra appeared to be 'amateurism at all cost.'

What it also did was to create great outrage in both Lancashire and Yorkshire particularly as it effectively meant that a club was considered to be guilty of professionalism and had then to prove its innocence. The side effect of this circular was that the attempts to examine charges of professionalism against the Lancashire senior clubs that Salford had raised had been put on hold until after that meeting down in London. On 6th November the Lancashire County Committee at a meeting stated they were to investigate the charges of professionalism made by the Salford Secretary Mr. Higson. They had decided that the first of those investigations would be against the Wigan club and would be held on the following Tuesday 13th November.

The meeting was held and the following day 14th November a detailed account of the investigation was carried by the Manchester Courier.[27] It was obvious just why Wigan had been put into the firing line from that report. It appeared that a Salford player named Miles had been approached by the Wigan club at the end of the 1893-94 season. It was alleged that following a meeting between the Wigan officials and Miles it was agreed that he would be paid thirty shillings per week throughout the summer on the understanding that he would then transfer to the Wigan club. When the new season arrived, Miles wrote to Wigan informing them he intended to remain at the Salford club.

At the hearing a witness claimed to have accompanied Miles to Wigan and on a number of occasions had been shown postal orders for thirty shillings reputedly from Wigan, by Miles. Wigan defended the charges stating no

---

[27] Manchester Courier 14th November 1894

payments had ever been made and that Mr Higson was simply being vindictive in making the allegations. After deliberating the matter, the committee decided Miles was guilty of professionalism and he was suspended sine-die. The Wigan club was also found guilty and suspended until 1st February 1895. It was a decision that added further fuel to the professional debate amongst the senior clubs in the county.

The issue of professionalism was not going away, rather, greater interest was being expressed in the newspapers, The Leeds Mercury on 19th November wrote:-[28]

**"And it becomes more and more evident that the future of the game depends very greatly upon the action taken by the leading clubs in Yorkshire and Lancashire for these counties are not only the two most powerful in the field at present, but their financial resources, if they are forced into an attitude of hostility to the Union would enable them to absorb whatever was worth buying in the rest of England. The Rugby Union would then become but a mere skeleton, which in a very few years would drop out of sight."**

It was a very powerful insight into the thinking of the senior clubs in the north. Financially they had so much clout they could afford to pay a great deal of money for any player in the country should professionalism be a road they wished to travel down. Equally newspapers

---

[28] Leeds Mercury 19th November 1894

were saying the problem was that clubs and officials in the south of the country had little or no idea of the situation in Lancashire and Yorkshire. They saw the problem as one of simple professionalism, if a man could not afford to play the game, then do not play. To the senior clubs in the north particularly in Yorkshire their power was blocked by the sheer number of lesser clubs throughout the county who could and would out vote them on any issue.

In Yorkshire the feeling was that clubs did not want professionalism in fact they felt it could not be afforded by any club. In Lancashire that was not the case, as we had seen clubs there were actively recruiting players from other clubs and even other countries in order to ensure promotion or stave off relegation. As the professionalism conflict grew we saw for the first time the thinking of the senior clubs as reported again in the Leeds Mercury on 3rd December, 1894:-[29]

**"If further conflict arises the Northern Clubs may secede and form a Northern Union. At the meetings of the Lancashire and Yorkshire Unions the question of professionalism has not been raised. But in Lancashire official circles, the feeling prevails that an adverse vote at the Rugby Union meeting would immediately bring forward counter-proposals."**

It was obvious just what those counter-proposals would be and that was, the formation of a breakaway

---

[29] Leeds Mercury 3rd December 1894

professional league. It was not a new concept in that county but it had never been so openly discussed before. The senior clubs particularly the ones in Lancashire were slowly but surely backing themselves into a corner. They were pushing the boundaries with regard to professionalism. As a result, Lancashire clubs were being fined and suspended which simply added fuel to the fire as far as the clubs were concerned. There was a growing belief that something had to give. As can be seen it was not broken time that was driving the clubs on but rather a desire to be fully professional in a manner similar to that model used by the Association Football Authorities.

As the year was coming to a close the events in regard to professionalism seemed to fade into the background a little whether by accident or design is difficult to ascertain. Certainly, news in the press was very scare on either the dispute in Yorkshire or professionalism in Lancashire.

# CHAPTER FOUR

## (1895)

It would be in the New Year that something concrete was reported on the progress made by the senior clubs. It fell to the Yorkshire Evening Post to publish details of the proposals on 14th January, 1895:-[30]

"**A meeting of the Committee of the Yorkshire Senior Competition has been called for tomorrow evening at the Green Dragon Hotel, Leeds. Among other items of business to be discussed is one described as 'The Lancashire and Yorkshire Senior Clubs.' This really involves a very important scheme. It is proposed to establish some sort of active connecting link between the leading clubs of Yorkshire and Lancashire, and whether that link is to take the form of an extended competition, a combined championship or a simple championship match between the winners of the Senior Competitions in the respective counties is a matter which is now under discussion. It will be well remembered that during the recent controversies on the professional question, the representatives of the Lancashire and Yorkshire Senior clubs held several meetings, and at one of these it was suggested that some basis of amalgamation should be agreed to, and that a common bond of interest between them should be formed.**"

---

[30] Yorkshire Evening Post 14th January 1895

The reporter went on to say that on 28th December, 1894, the clubs had held a meeting and decided that each county should set up a sub-committee to talk over these issues. While the Yorkshire clubs had still to form such a sub-committee the Lancashire clubs had one in place and were eager to forward matters. This was the first indication that the clubs in the two counties were preparing to join forces in a hope that their relative positions would be strengthened with regard to the authorities. As is ever the case in rugby league then as now the urge to complicate matters was strong. One of the suggestions under consideration was to select from the 'pick' of the clubs in both counties and the suggestion was four from each competition should form a separate competition in each county the winner of which would be classed as the champion club of Lancashire and Yorkshire. No one mentioned just which clubs would be the 'pick' of each competition or how that selection process would work.

The problems was, that particularly in Yorkshire the only way a club could accommodate eight extra matches would be by resigning from the Yorkshire Cup Competition. The other alternative would be to give up every other fixture outside the Yorkshire Senior Competition. There was another complication, namely the proposal by the Rugby Union to shorten the existing season by two weeks at the beginning and end of the season. What was important however, was the possibility of a stronger bond between the two organisations and that would undoubtably cause problems with the Rugby Union according to the reporter:-

**"In view of the obvious hostility towards Northern football clubs that exists in the South of England, the clubs in Lancashire and Yorkshire feel that it is absolutely necessary some joint organisation should be formed by which their interests may be mutually protected."**

The reporter went on to report that the sub-committees would draw up some scheme whereby the senior clubs would control their own destiny while not being antagonistic towards the Rugby Union governing bodies. However, as he put it:-

**"It will be a practical evidence of the fact that the leading clubs of Lancashire and Yorkshire are henceforth determined to support each other at all costs and against all comers."**

There is little doubt that the clubs were throwing down the gauntlet not only to their respective county unions but also the Rugby Union authorities down in London. At this time antagonism toward clubs in the north of the country from clubs particularly in the south was growing. It was now becoming inevitable that trouble between all parties involved could not be avoided, the question was just when that conflict would erupt and what form it would take.

During January and February, the Lancashire and Yorkshire clubs continued with their separate plans and ideas as to what was the best way forward. A joint meeting was proposed to establish a Northern League. Down in London the authorities held their own meeting to try to decide just what action to take with regard to the formation of any new Northern League. A motion was proposed that the Union should prohibit the formation of any Union or League of the nature being proposed by the senior clubs in both counties. They could not decide on an appropriate action so postposed any decision to a later meeting. What was obvious was the Union was not going to tamely succumb to the demands of the northern clubs. The problem was the authorities had little or no idea just what the clubs in the north were actually proposing.

The clubs themselves called yet another meeting which they did not publicise, at which they discussed their plans to form a new Northern Union League. This was in spite of the English Rugby Union indicating quite firmly that they would not be prepared to support such a move. There were two separate approaches if the truth be told. The Lancashire clubs who were suffering greater from suspensions due to professionalism breaches were favouring a league that would be out and out professional with players being paid openly. In Yorkshire the clubs were leaning more toward maintaining the status quo and continuing to pay the illegal broken time payments which hopefully would eventually be legitimised by the authorities. Also, they wanted support for their growing demands that they be allowed to run the Alliance League as they saw fit. Their aim was to get all the clubs in both counties to present a united front against the authorities both in the counties and the country.

In Yorkshire the authorities were aware of the club's stand and had made arrangements with their counterparts in Lancashire regarding any new league. They according to the Yorkshire Evening Post on 19th February, 1895 had decided that the sanctioning of any new combination would have to be left to the Committee of the English Union.[31] They also went on to say that the English Rugby Union would need to be fully aware of and convinced about, as they put it the *bona-fides* of the new organisation. In other words, the county unions were attempting to abdicate responsibility for dealing with the senior clubs on this matter.

What was worrying the authorities was simply the fact the senior clubs were holding meetings in both counties in secret. What was common knowledge was that the clubs wanted to set up a new league encompassing clubs from both counties. The clubs had however not approached the authorities asking for permission to do so, neither had they provided a list of rules or bye-laws for the new set up. More worrying still was the growing belief that the clubs had entered into a secret agreement

---

[31] Yorkshire Evening Post 19th February 1895

and the Yorkshire Evening Post alluded to this in the article on 19th February:-

**"The published objects of which the Union is being formed consists of the 'furthering of the interests of Rugby football,' the playing of an inter-championship match, and the acceptance of a hard and fast transfer law. It is understood, however, that beneath these objects there is an agreement which has not seen the light, and it is this agreement that members of the Rugby Union Committee vainly sought information about when the question was recently before them. We may say that the secret contract, so called, consists of a provision under which all of the clubs are bound to stand by each other in the event of a disagreement with the Rugby Union. If one club is brought up for professionalism and treated with unfairness or harshness, the remaining clubs will investigate its case and stand by it, face the Rugby Union, and take the consequences."**

The clubs claimed that this agreement was as a result of the now discredited memorandum from the Rugby Union whereby clubs had to prove their innocence published back in late December. The question that needed to be asked was why were the clubs wanting to come into conflict with the authorities. What they wanted was to be able to play each other and the champion club in the two counties would play each other for the championship. To accomplish this there was no need to seek approval from either the county or national authorities. All that was needed was for the clubs to arrange fixtures with each other. After all such leagues already existed in the two counties but on a smaller scale.

The clubs however, had another agenda namely, in Lancashire the desire to make any such league professional and its players paid openly. In Yorkshire on the other hand, the senior clubs were determined to take full control of the Senior Competition and refuse to allow promotion or relegation except under their terms. They wanted similar control over any newly formed northern league. Both organisations were 'tilting at windmills' simply because way back in 1892 the Rugby Union had refused to sanction any such action in either county. The clubs were not prepared to back down on these issues. What they still failed to recognise was the shift in support within the counties. Back in 1892 the vast majority of clubs and supporters in Yorkshire favoured the senior clubs' ambitions. Many were in favour of the county setting up a league system. They had even been supportive of the broken time issue the county had put forward to the authorities in 1893. By 1895 the reverse was the case, the senior clubs were now seen as not wanting to further the game but simply protect their own interests.

As March came in once again the Rugby Union was meeting and, on the agenda, yet again was the proposed new league. They were becoming more exasperated at the lack of information the senior clubs were providing to them and to their respective county authorities. The Birmingham Daily Post on Saturday 9th March reported. [32]

**"The proposed Northern League again came under discussion and the committee passed the following resolution. That unless the proposed League of Yorkshire and Lancashire clubs submit their bye-laws and objects to the Rugby Union Committee before April 30th negotiations toward formation will be forbidden."**

There was no doubt that battle lines were being drawn by both sides in the dispute. In the middle of March, the Yorkshire Second Competition Committee approached the committee of the Senior Competition asking specifically for a copy of their bye-laws including bye-law number 28. They were preparing to press for a Test match between the top club of the second division and bottom club of the first division as per that bye-law. The big question all were asking was simple, would the senior clubs comply with their own bye-law or again re-elect the bottom two clubs.

The Leeds Mercury on 15th March wrote of the events ongoing over the Pennines.[33]

**"The clubs in this competition are determined that they will work the same without being under the control of the County Committee and the latter have**

---
[32] Birmingham Daily Post 9th March 1895
[33] Leeds Mercury 15th March 1895

**been asked to agree to them doing so. On Wednesday night there was a representative gathering of the organisations concerned at which a proposed set of rules was framed. These will come under the consideration of the Lancashire County Committee in a few days and it is confidently expected they will be consented to."**

In truth there was no way the Lancashire authorities could agree to the demands, the precedent for refusing such a move had been set back in 1892 by the Rugby Union. It is interesting to note just who was the ad-hoc secretary and spokesman for the Lancashire clubs at this time. It was none other than Joseph Platt of the Oldham club, one of the leaders in the attempts to form a professional organisation. He was obviously feeding information from his own or the Oldham clubs' agenda on this issue to reporters who were printing what he said quite readily.

Throughout March of that year the clubs particularly in Lancashire were become more and more belligerent towards both the county and national authorities. They were now talking about openly defying the authorities should they not get their own demands met. It was a subtle but significant change from standing together should a club be punished by the authorities to now being determined to refuse to obey the authorities. On Wednesday 20th March yet another meeting of the clubs was held at the George Hotel in Huddersfield, it was called to discuss the new rules for the proposed new northern league before submitting them to the authorities. It appeared that no decision was agreed on and the meeting adjourned to a later date.

While all seemed to be going well with the proposals for the new league the increased aggression toward the Rugby Union was beginning to cause a number of clubs in both counties some concern. It is worth noting that coverage of events in the newspapers was far greater over in Yorkshire than it was in Lancashire. In the latter country the newspapers were more concerned with the rival code of soccer. It was hardly surprising given that in the Football League first division six of the clubs were Lancashire based while in Yorkshire it was only Sheffield United and The Wednesday club. The sporting articles in newspapers leaned more to the goings on of the soccer clubs than the now fading rugby union clubs as they saw it.

It was the Yorkshire Evening Post that first published the bombshell with regard to the proposed new Northern League. If all thought the new league was sailing long the reporter dispelled that notion.[34] He revealed that three of the Yorkshire clubs in the senior competition were discussing the possibility of withdrawing from the new League. The three were Leeds, Bradford and Huddersfield, Leeds did have history as they had done the same thing when matters got difficult back in 1892.

---

[34] Yorkshire Evening Post 28th March 1895

It was also rumoured that Halifax were somewhat undecided in their support for the new league.

The talk in the county was that should the three clubs go through with their intentions other clubs would be only too willing to step in and replace then. The likes of Leeds Parish Church and Castleford were mentioned. That being the case the feeling was the new proposals were not under threat. The question however was why, why would three clubs wish to withdraw at this stage. The problem got worse for the new league when the following day the Leeds Mercury reported:-[35]

**"Considerably more is being made of a threatened split among the clubs who propose to form a Northern Rugby League than the circumstances warrant. All the clubs concerned came to a clear understanding to stand together, and, if we are not mistaken, an undertaking to that effect was signed by a representative of each, but no pledge was extracted that action should be taken in common in defiance of the Rugby Union should that body prove hostile."**

So, while the clubs were prepared to support each other some were not prepared to support any action that was in defiance of Union rules. The reporter went on to state that:-

**"It never has been either the wish or the policy of the Yorkshiremen to needlessly get into conflict with the**

---

[35] Leeds Mercury 29th March 1895

**Rugby Union officials, and while they are desirous of effecting an alliance with the leading Lancashire organisations, they are not prepared to raise the standard of revolt except in defence of their own existence, or when a principle is at stake."**

It is hard to understand just what that statement meant but it appears they did not want to upset the Union so long as the clubs could get their own way. Should they not then they were prepared to take action. It could also be interpreted as being they were not prepared to support the Lancashire clubs over the issue of professionalism. What was evident was that cracks were appearing in the unity of the senior clubs in both counties. Those cracks seemingly got wider when the same paper reported that both Salford and Swinton were expressing opposition to the scheme. They were joined by Barrow who were to join the first division come the following season along with Broughton Rangers. The whole scheme was in danger of collapse and was only being kept afloat according to the reporter by two Lancashire clubs:-

**"The scheme, as a matter of fact, would have dropped at once so far as Lancashire is concerned, but for the action of Oldham and Warrington and the first named of the pair have been particularly pressing in their actions."**

The secretary of the Oldham club at this time was as stated earlier was Joseph Platt. So, the question is just what was causing this change of heart by at least five

Lancashire clubs and three in Yorkshire. The answer can be found in the Manchester Courier the following day 30th March. The newspaper actually listed the resolutions the clubs had been discussing for weeks.[36]

"1. That the premier clubs of Lancashire and Yorkshire as here represented do form themselves into a Union for the purpose of furthering the interests of Rugby Football in the two counties.

2. That the Union be governed by one representative of each club, the officials to consist of President, Vice– President, Hon Secretary and Treasurer to be selected from such representatives.

3. That the champion club of the first division of the Lancashire club championship and the champion club of the Yorkshire senior competition play a match for the championship of the Union.

4Any bone-fide playing member of a club shall be eligible to play with any club in this Union provided he has not taken part in a match already with another club in this Union. If he has so played permission for his transfer must be obtained from the club he has played for and be sanctioned by the committee.

5. In the event of any club in the Union being expelled or in any way punished by the English Rugby Union

---

[36] Manchester Courier 30th March 1895

**or their representative county union club shall have right to appeal to this committee."**

On first viewing it seemed there was again nothing untoward in the resolutions however, it was resolution five that was causing a good number of clubs problems. It gave the new Northern Union the right to countermand any decision of the Rugby Union against a club in the Union. The proposed Northern Union was in fact still wanting to control its own affairs while continuing to be a member of the Rugby Union. Many in the game knew very well that was not possible simply because the English Rugby Union had ruled that the Yorkshire Alliance could not go ahead way back in 1892. Therefore, many felt the new Northern Union was not going to be sanctioned either. Also, many clubs were not prepared to disobey the Rugby Union.

For this reason, many reporters were coming to the opinion that the proposed Lancashire and Yorkshire Union was now bound to fail. They and many supporters could not see with at least five Lancashire clubs and three from Yorkshire possibly more not prepared to go against the authorities how the proposals could go ahead. The likes of Joseph Platt of the Oldham club and some of the more vocal Lancashire clubs had differing views and were still determined to continue and push forward with the venture.

To that end yet another meeting was called in Huddersfield with the aim once again of drafting a set of rules for the new venture. The reporter for the Leeds Mercury felt that rather than writing rules they could well be writing the funeral rites for the Union.[37]

**"..but is as much as success was entirely dependent upon complete accord in principle and absolute unity of action- which unfortunately, are conspicuously absent- it may be taken for granted that tonight's meeting will merely perform the funeral obsequies of a body which ceased to exist almost as soon as it was born. The action taken by sundry Lancashire clubs as once more proved that these are wax in the heads of the county's representatives on the Rugby Union Committee, to be moulded practically as they please, while coincident with their defection has been the far more damaging secession of the Leeds, Bradford and Huddersfield clubs."**

There was little doubt that the results from that meeting on 3rd April would have been eagerly awaited by reporters and supporters alike. What was decided upon would shape the future of the game itself not only in the two counties but also the country.

The Liverpool Mercury carried an article on 4th April with regard to that meeting at the George Hotel. Contrary to expectations rather that holding the last rites for the venture the opposite occurred in so much as the clubs actually put together a comprehensive set of rules for the venture. Not only that but the clubs present

---

[37] Leeds Mercury 3rd April 1895

actually voted to adopt them and the newspaper published those rules.[38]

"The following rules were adopted

1. That the union be called The Lancashire and Yorkshire Rugby Football Union of Senior Clubs.

2. That the union be a member of the English Rugby Union.

3. That the union be governed by one representative from each club the officials consisting of President Vice-President Hon. Secretary and Treasurer to be selected from such representatives.

4. That the officials be elected annually at a meeting of the representatives of each club in the union such meetings being held alternately in Lancashire and Yorkshire.

5. That the annual subscription to the union be one guinea payable not later than September one in each year.

6. That a committee of management be elected consisting of eight members four from each county five members to form a quorum.

7. That the Hon. Secretary shall call a special meeting on receipt of a request to do so signed by at least eight members.

---

[38] Liverpool Mercury 4th April 1895

8. That the Hon. Secretary shall receive the subscriptions and all monies accruing to the union and shall keep proper accounts of the same, such accounts to be audited every season by two honorary auditors appointed by the committee.

9. That the champion club in the first division of the Lancashire Club Championship and the champion club of the Yorkshire Senior Competition play a match for the championship of the union.

10. Any bone-fide member of a club shall be eligible to play for any club in the union. Provided he has not taken part in a match already with another club in the union. If he has so played permission for his transfer must be obtained from the club for which he has played and he must in addition have obtained the sanction of the committee of this union.

11. The committee have the power to deal with any offending club or clubs as they may think fit, and shall have the power to deal with any matter that arises in connection with the union and that is not provided for in these rules.

It was resolved that a copy of the rules of this union be sent to the Yorkshire and Lancashire County Committees and that they be informed that it had been the intention of this union to have submitted the rules to them but having received from an intimation from Mr. Rowland Hill that it is necessary to submit the rules direct to the English Rugby Union, a copy of

**the rules now adopted be forwarded for the English Rugby Union's approval."**

The rules were simply a rehash and extension of those published earlier in the Manchester newspaper. This time it was rule number 11 that was going to cause a problem simply because it would be read as usurping the authority of both the national and county bodies. What it did do however, was reveal that the clubs were now determined to continue with the plan to set up their own league. All that could be done now, was to sit back and await the rulings from the two county unions and the Rugby Union on the proposals. It would be May before any further news was forthcoming to the senior clubs.

Over in Lancashire the senior clubs were becoming more and more belligerent toward the authorities. They via Joseph Platt had driven through plans for a new league. Bolstered by that they were now casting envious eyes at the power the Yorkshire clubs possessed. There clubs had successfully warded off any action from the Yorkshire rugby union authorities with regard to the dispute about Castleford and their refusal to allow that club into the senior competition. The Lancashire clubs were after the same powers over their league and wanted them immediately. The reason for this was that Barrow had won the second division and therefore would play in the first division in the coming season. A number of the clubs stated quite categorically that they would not play Barrow and wanted them replaced by Widnes. The Widnes club had finished in third spot but they were much closer to the rest of the clubs than was a long trip up to Cumberland. That coupled with the prospect of a larger fan base made that club a more profitable option. The authorities of course refused to sanction such a move and that further angered the senior clubs.

On 10th May the Rugby Union met in London and discussed amongst other things the proposed new league. They considered the rules and objects sent to them and then passed the following resolution which was reported the following day:-[39]

**"This committee, being of opinion that any such organisation as the proposed union of Lancashire and Yorkshire clubs would be prejudicial to the best interests of the game. Forbids the formation of such union."**

It was a bitter blow to the new league as the controlling body for the game in England was refusing to sanction them. The knock-on effect from this was that both the Lancashire and Yorkshire authorities were bound to support the Rugby Union rather than the senior clubs. This the Lancashire authorities had officially done on 17th April while Yorkshire had followed suit on 22nd April. You would have thought that there the matter would rest however, that proved not to be the case. Also, in Yorkshire yet another dispute was coming to a head. By their prevaricating the senior clubs had managed to stave off any punitive action from the authorities over

---

[39] Manchester Courier 11th May 1895

their decision not to admit Castleford to the senior competition for the 1893-94 season. As the 1894-95 season had come to a close the second division had been won by Morley and they approached the Yorkshire Rugby Union demanding they be allowed to play a 'Test' match against the bottom club in the senior competition as per bye-law 28 of the Senior Competition rules.

The senior clubs for their part while not refusing simply sat back and did nothing, after all such stalling tactics had been successful for the past twelve months so why not adopt them again. The problem was that the authorities were growing increasingly frustrated with the behaviour of the senior clubs but more importantly so were the rest of the clubs in the county, the reporters covering the game and the supporters. It was a complete reversal of the situation just three years previous.

On 27th May the Yorkshire County authorities met at Green Dragon Hotel, in Leeds. On the agenda was the passing of the minutes from the Senior Competition as had been required since 1892. One of the questioned raised at the meeting was reported in the Leeds Mercury the following day. It referred to the constitution of the Senior Competition for the 1894-95 season and was causing great concern for the authorities. Some present felt that the time had come to do something definite about the promotion and relegation issue. The authorities had been told in the past to wait until the end of the season, that had come and gone and a settlement of the problem was no nearer. A Mr Tattersall stated:-[40]

**"...it is time the matter was settled. The Senior Competition had put the matter off from time to time, and it looked as if they were trying to shelve the matter until the present committee were out of office."**

A great deal of discussion followed with both the authorities and representatives from the clubs having their say on matters. The authorities were insisting the clubs state their intentions to them by 1st June. The clubs felt not for the first time that the authorities were trying to dictate to them. Eventually the following resolution was adopted:-

**"That the secretary be instructed to write to the Senior Competition requesting a definite reply with regard to the constitution of the Senior Competition for the season 1895-96 on or before Saturday 1st June."**

While some at the meeting were worried about dictating to the senior clubs a Mr Gladstone had other ideas and perhaps summed up the feelings of many in the county stating:-

---

[40] Leeds Mercury 28th May 1895

**"...it was time the Senior Competition were told what they ought to do- they had ignored the committee long enough."**

The day of reckoning was fast approaching for all concerned in the growing dispute in the county.

Just two days later on 30th May the senior clubs met at the Green Dragon Hotel this time knowing very well that pressure was mounting on them. There was growing anger toward the senior clubs not only from the two northern counties but also from the rest of the authorities throughout the country. That anger centred on the club's refusal to respond to the edicts from both county authorities and also the Rugby Union. Equally, increasing was the anger of supporters who saw the clubs simply looking after their own self interests.

On the following day the Yorkshire Evening Post covered the meeting of the clubs. The reporter mentioned the term 'promotion on merit' controversy and that it was resulting in serious conflict between the two protagonists. He also simply and clearly laid out the facts writing:-[41]

**"The dispute between the two bodies which occurred last autumn will be well remembered by football readers. That dispute had reference to the acceptance, by means of a test match of the No. 2 winners in the senior ranks. The Senior Competition**

---

[41] Yorkshire Evening Post 31st May 1895

**Committee stated they accepted the principle, but declined to agree to a hard and fast rule on the subject, after they had formally given in their adhesion to it and given the Second Competition Committee a written undertaking that in future a match between the Senior lowest and the second highest club should take place each year. The controversy has lain dormant for some months, but it has now broken out with redoubled force. The Yorkshire Union at their meeting last Monday discussed the matter, and gave a plain intimation that the Senior Competition Committee must decide the whole question of promotion by merit before Saturday, June 1."**

It is worth noting here that nowhere was there any mention of the dispute in Yorkshire being in any way connected with the issue of broken time payments to players. This was the argument put forward at the now famous meeting at the George Hotel as being the reason for the split from the parent body. At the meeting the senior clubs discussed the matter and met a deputation from the two lowest clubs Hull and Wakefield. Those clubs pressed their claim to be re-elected to the senior competition. They then met a deputation from the Second Competition at which they were presented with a copy of the letter stating that a Test match would take place between the top of their competition and the bottom of the senior competition.

The deputation expressed the view that the letter from the clubs had never been withdrawn and asked the senior clubs to either carry out what they had agreed to or state definitely arrangements with regard to the future. Mr Collins one of the deputation from the second competition stated that as he refereed games he had often seen Morley the winner of the second competition play. He went on to say:-

**"It had been hinted that the Seniors might object to take in any club from the Second rank, on the grounds of unsuitability of style of play, and he proceeded to deal with Morley's claims in this respect when his remarks were cut short by the committee and stated to be unnecessary."**

With the deputations now withdrawing the clubs discussed the situation in private and shortly afterwards made the following announcement:-

**"That the Hull F.C. and Wakefield Trinity F.C. be re-admitted to the Senior Competition for the season 1895-96."**

While this resolution was then communicated to the two clubs the delegation from the second competition who had been told a decision would be communicated to them heard nothing. Not only that they actually left the meeting not knowing just what the intentions of the senior clubs was with regard to the Morley club. They were less than pleased and also told the reporter that their reception by the senior clubs had been less cordial than it should have been. The clubs had actually broken their own bye-law which that had agreed to which had stated:-

**"That next season the bottom club in the Senior Competition shall retire and play the winner of the Competition No.2 a deciding match, the winning club in such match to be included in the Senior Competition for the season following."**

The clubs also took no official notice of the intimation from the Yorkshire Rugby Union regarding promotion on merit and their need to inform the authorities of their intentions by 1st June. When the reporter pressed them on the matter, they simply stated that they had no information to communicate. The reaction was predictable and the reporter stated:-

**"Very strong exception is taken in nearly all football circles at the persistent way in which the claims of the Second Competition have been trifled with, and the feeling is shared by many men of standing and influence in the Senior clubs themselves. It is felt that by their repeated 'shuffling' – a better word could hardly be used – the Competition Committee have shown that they desire not so much the general welfare of Yorkshire football as the maintenance of their own clubs as a closed corporation. This the Yorkshire Union and the general clubs of the county are not likely to quietly agree to, and they will now be fortified in dealing with the question by the**

**knowledge of the fact that public opinion almost unanimously condemns the attitude which the Senior Competition Committee have taken up."**

If there was one moment in this whole sorry saga that one could say the senior clubs had burned their boats, this was it. The upcoming AGM of the Yorkshire Union was fast approaching and they would most certainly have been forced into taking stronger action against the senior outfits.

If the senior clubs thought the rest of the clubs in the county were about to sit back and await action from the authorities they were mistaken. The Hull Daily Mail just five days later reported on the junior club's actions.[42] They reported that the clubs in the second competition had organised a meeting for the 6th June at the Wellington Hotel, Leeds. They invited clubs from the third and fourth competition along with any other clubs affiliated to the Yorkshire Rugby Union. Quite pointedly the senior clubs were not invited.

The purpose of the meeting was to discuss a motion to **'pledge not to vote for the election of the Senior Competition representatives on the Yorkshire Union.'** The clubs were intending to remove the senior clubs or their representatives from being elected on to the Yorkshire Rugby Union Committee at the upcoming Union AGM. It was a very clever move as if adhered to it would hamstring the senior clubs attempts to

---

[42] Hull Daily Mail 3rd June 1895

prevaricate as they had been doing for the past twelve months or more. The reason for this was the senior clubs would have no representative on the committee to put forward their claims. Also their voting power on that committee would be greatly reduced.

The Yorkshire Evening Post on 7th June reported on that meeting. The reporter stated that the clubs were prepared to put up a stubborn fight in their determination to obtain promotion on merit throughout the county. The meeting asked that the Yorkshire County Committee prove itself to be the supreme authority in the county football and do so by requiring the rulers of the Senior Competition to conform to the rules on which it was established. The meeting also reiterated the fact that unlike in 1892 when the senior clubs had full support now the opposite was the case.

The reporter went on to state with regard to the senior clubs:-[43]

**"They seemed to think that Yorkshire consisted of twelve clubs and nobody else, and that they should rule whether it served the interests of the county or not."**

There was a feeling at the meeting that a crisis could be avoided simply because the senior clubs when they saw that the rest of Yorkshire was opposed to them would come to their senses. It was a view that ultimately would

---

[43] Yorkshire Evening Post 7th June 1895

prove to be wrong. The meeting did pass the resolution mentioned earlier that the committee exercise their authority and bring the senior clubs into line.

Over in Lancashire the clubs there were watching on with interest at the events in Yorkshire. There was a growing envy within some clubs of the power their Yorkshire rivals seemingly possessed and it would appear intended to retain. There was a little coterie of clubs with opposition toward Barrow the newly elected club to the first division along with both Salford and Swinton who were not in favour of opposing the authority of the Rugby Union. The question needing to be asked was simply, just what was the thinking of the senior clubs in both counties. This coupled with the fact the senior competition was now in disarray following the suspension of three of the Lancashire clubs was angering the clubs.

Since the early days back toward the end of 1892 both county unions had reservations and opposition to the formation of a new league. The Rugby Union had specifically refused to endorse the Yorkshire club's demands. At the present time Joseph Platt had received a letter from the Rugby Union in reply to his sending of the rules and objects of the proposed new northern league that read:-

**"Dear sir, - My committee have considered your letter stating the objects and also the rules of the proposed union of Lancashire and Yorkshire senior**

**clubs, and their regret that they are unable to sanction the formation of such a body. At their meeting held last night, the following resolution was adopted: - 'This committee being of opinion that any such organisation as the proposed union of Lancashire and Yorkshire clubs would be prejudicial to the best interests of the game, forbids the formation of such a union.' – Yours truly G. Rowland Hill."**

Given such a ruling it is hard to see how the senior clubs persisted with the idea that they could rely on the protection of the Rugby Union regarding their dispute with their respective county unions. It could not have been made any clearer the formation of a new league would not receive official sanction. That was perhaps what was driving Barrow, Salford and Swinton to their conclusions. It would also colour the thinking of a number of Yorkshire clubs in the coming days.

The Yorkshire AGM was held on 17th June and was as to be expected a lively affair. The main business was the dispute with the senior clubs over their decision to decline to recognise the claim of the Second Competition winners to be promoted. The meeting resolved **'that the Senior Clubs must declare their lowest club from the previous season by 1st July and that such lowest club must play Morley, the Second Competition winners between September 21st and 28th, the winner to be include in the Senior Competition for next season.'**

The Yorkshire Rugby Union was throwing the gauntlet down at long last, there was little else they could do such was the depth of feeling from the rest of the clubs in the county. The Senior clubs for their part were determined to withstand the onslaught come what may and their response was reported by the Huddersfield Chronicle on 22nd June.[44] Put simply their decision was to defy the Yorkshire Union all of the senior clubs decided they would not accede to the request made regarding promotion and relegation. Not only that they reserved the right to itself the power, as originally given by the Yorkshire authorities when the new league was constituted back in 1892. The reporter expressed the view that the resolution would be adhered to even though it may well lead to the expulsion of the clubs from the English Union.

From that it would be safe to assume the clubs knew very well that expulsion from the county union meant expulsion from the Rugby Union. They did also do what they had done since their very existence, namely to send two delegated to the proposed meeting by the authorities to discuss promotion and relegation issues. The meeting was to be held in the coming days and the clubs were determined to have their say when it took place. Their actions were perhaps pre-empted by what happened over the Pennines as June came to its close.

---

[44] Huddersfield Chronicle 22nd June 1895

There was a great deal of evidence that the Lancashire clubs were becoming even more aggressive in their dealing with the county authorities than were their Yorkshire counterparts. It is difficult to say why that was but perhaps it was the urging of the likes of Joseph Platt from the Oldham club in his capacity as secretary of the ad-hoc groups of Lancashire clubs. One thing was certain it was the Lancashire clubs that were to take decisive action first as June came to its end. Strangely enough it was a Lancashire newspaper, the Manchester Courier that broke the news to supporters.[45]

**"A subject which is engaging a good deal of attention just now in Rugby football circles is the resignation of nine out of the 12 clubs who are included in the Senior Competition, of the Lancashire County Football Clubs. The organisations which have thought it desirable to take this course are, Broughton Rangers, Oldham, Wigan, Warrington, Tyldesley, St. Helens, Leigh, Rochdale Hornets and Widnes, and the three clubs that have declined to join them are Barrow, Salford and Swinton. In this matter certain differences which have existed between the County Committee and the seceding clubs have been brought to a culminating point. The differences relate chiefly to the government of the competition, the selection of referees and some minor details. The wish of the discontents is that the clubs engaging in the competition should have control of it,**

---

[45] Manchester Courier 4th July 1895

**including the power of nominating the referees as well as discretion in other details: The County Committee on the other hand wisely think that the interests of the game will be best served if they retain the management of the contest in their own hands. The dissatisfaction which exists is not, it is stated, confined to the organisation above named, for they have received assurances of support from a number of clubs engaged in the second and third competitions in an attempt to alter the existing conditions. It has been reported that the seceders intend to form another competition with the name of the Lancashire First Class Rugby Clubs Championship Committee; that the membership be limited to 12 and the management vested in a committee of that number and composed of one representative from each club."**

The major shock to supporters of the game would have been the fact that two of the most powerful clubs in the county in Salford and Swinton had chosen not to resign. Barrow as a newly elected member of the senior competition were hardly likely to elect not to take part having won promotion. As we shall see later both powerful outfits would have a change of heart once it became obvious the county authorities were intending to continue with a weakened first division. The quality of opposition Salford and Swinton would meet following the split would prove to be far too weak to attract any worthwhile support and that meant financial disaster.

There is little doubt that the similarity of the desires of the clubs in both counties resulted in a good number of 'secret' meetings between the two bodies. The article went on to state that the Lancashire clubs also wanted to abolish the existing first division competition should they succeed in their demands. If the Lancashire clubs were still of the opinion they could shelter under the protection of the English Rugby Union the reporter dispelled that notion writing:-

**"The rules of the Rugby Union do not permit a combination of clubs without their sanction and if a counter combination were started it is, in the last degree improbable that the Union would approve of it while that under the control of the County Committee is in existence."**

One has to wonder just what it would take for the clubs to understand or accept that whatever they were proposing the Rugby Union was never going to sanction it. Still the clubs in both counties continued down the path they were on. Perhaps they had gone so far that it was now impossible for them to stop or even change course. On the other hand, perhaps, they were hell bent on generating a confrontation that would lead to a breakaway.

Just a few days later the Yorkshire County Committee met yet again in Leeds to consider the action or should that be lack of action by the senior clubs. The crux of the dispute for the clubs was that when the Senior

Competition had been established it was their contention that the power to decide what clubs would constitute the competition was delegated to them by the authorities. The Yorkshire authorities contended that was true but only for the first season and concerned those first ten clubs. Rather than prevaricate any further the Yorkshire Committee took the decision to withdraw the powers delegated to the senior clubs. In essence they used the clause in the settlement arrangements back in August 1892 and agreed to by the clubs which stated:-

**'Whilst delegating these powers the Yorkshire Rugby Football Union reserve to themselves the right at any time to adjudicate on any question which may arise on an appeal being made to them and shall have full power to alter or over-ride the decision of the sub-committee.'**

They were at last exercising the very power of veto they had given to themselves and in effect abolished the Senior Competition. The clubs were now left with nowhere to go and were forced once again to meet to decide on their next course of action. They still had not read the mood of the rugby world in the county, or perhaps they had and did not give a damn. They met on Friday 19th July at the Mitre Hotel in Leeds and at the meeting the twelve clubs of the senior competition tendered their resignation from the Yorkshire County Rugby Union. The Leeds Times carried an account of the meeting the following day writing:-[46]. After a long discussion the following resolution was passed: -

"Owing to the action of the Yorkshire Rugby Union Committee at their meeting on July 8th, 1895, withdrawing powers delegated to the Yorkshire Senior Competition, the twelve clubs here represented withdraw their membership from the Yorkshire Rugby Union."

The article went on to outline the club's chief complaint simply that they were inadequately represent on the County Committee and as a result were at the mercy of the junior clubs. Each club had an equal voice and vote and so the junior clubs were masters of the situation. The clubs again reiterated the view that they would be able to shelter under the protection of the English Rugby Union. That would, they claimed enable then to arrange matches with each other and any other clubs as they saw fit. It is difficult to see just how that view could possibly still prevail given the communications they had received from the Rugby Union. It is also interesting to note that the clubs resigned in July not the end of August that we are led to believe.

There was no way the Rugby Union was going to alter its stance as there was a growing feeling in the south of the country that semi-professionalism in the form of broken time payments was rife in Lancashire and Yorkshire and this was just another step down the road to full professionalism. Many felt it would be better to let the whole of Lancashire and Yorkshire and their

---

[46] Leeds Times 20th July 1895

county unions go rather than keep them as **'a spreading ulcer in amateur football'**. Given all of these views just why the senior clubs decided to continue with their belief is difficult to comprehend. Most certainly it was a very brave decision or perhaps a foolish one but continue on they did along with the Lancashire clubs. Perhaps that had been their intention all along and they were happy to have generated the conflict they did. There were now twenty one senior clubs from both counties that were no longer members of the Rugby Union.

On the other hand, perhaps the Yorkshire clubs felt the Yorkshire Union would capitulate once again as they had in 1892. Back then the authorities had been very jealous of their position as the premier county in the country, a county that won the County Championship with monotonous regularity. That was back then, now such was the depth of ill feeling toward the senior clubs from the whole of the county it would have been a brave committeeman who suggested backing down now. Having communicated their resignation to the Yorkshire authorities the clubs sat back and awaited the response from that direction, they did not have that long to wait and it was not what they would have wanted to hear.

On Monday 29th July the Yorkshire Rugby Union Committee met in Leeds. A lengthy discussion took place we are told, as to what should be done with regard to the resignations of the senior clubs. Mr. Waller the former President of the Union when asked, could give no comment as to why the resignations had been issued. It was pointed out by some that the lack of representation on the committee from the senior clubs was but a secondary complaint and one the authorities were powerless to address. After all they were not in a position to instruct clubs just how they should cast their vote at an AGM. It was also pointed out that at the last committee meeting the senior clubs had made no mention of this issue.

One of the committeemen wanted a full discussion before the resignations were accepted. His argument was that the twelve senior clubs had been pioneers for the game in Yorkshire. In addition, they had consistently supplied the players for county games and their grounds had also hosted many of those county games. He felt the clubs deserved a fuller hearing. The counter argument was that of the twelve clubs that had resigned only two had given reasons in their letter of resignation. Hunslet stated they had resigned in accordance with the actions of other senior clubs. Liversedge stated they were leaving due to the actions of the Yorkshire Union against the senior clubs.

The conclusions arrived at by the committee were that the senior club's main complaint was solely and simply about the issue of promotion by merit. If the clubs continued on the path they were on, they could find their interests would suffer. Not only that but if they were disposed to come back into the Rugby Union, they may well find the terms for such a return much harder that they had at present. It was a veiled threat and one which did not go unnoticed by the clubs. The Committee were all sorry that the clubs had seceded from the union but felt the clubs had no defence for their action. As a result, the feeling was they could do nothing but accept the resignations tendered by the twelve clubs. When the vote was taken it was carried by a vote of ten to three. So, as of 29th July the twelve senior clubs joined their Lancashire counterparts as outcasts from the Rugby Union. This was a full month before the date we are led to believe such action occurred!

So, they joined the senior outfits over in Lancashire in leaving their county unions but refused to accept the obvious that they were also now also outcasts from the English Rugby Union. If there was any doubt regarding this fact it was dispelled following a meeting of the English Rugby Union in London on 9th August. At that meeting the committee passed the following resolution.[47]

**"That this committee confirms the action taken by the Yorkshire County Committee in withdrawing the powers formerly given to the Senior Competition."**

Having thrown their support in favour of the county authorities there was no doubt they would have also taken the view the senior clubs were now no longer members of the Rugby Union. All the clubs were now in limbo and further backed into a corner by their own actions. The question now presenting itself was just what was the way forward if any. The York Herald of 14th

---

[47] Leeds Times 10 August 1895

August gave a good indication of the thinking of the Yorkshire senior clubs.[48]

**"Although the Yorkshire Rugby Union have withdrawn the powers originally granted the clubs in the Senior Competition the latter still continue to hold meetings to discuss the situation. A private meeting of the senior club representatives was held at the Mitre Hotel, Leeds, last evening and lasted close upon three hours, the press representatives present being informed at the conclusion that there was nothing connected with the meeting to be communicated. In the meantime, arbitration is being spoken of as the best means of bringing about a solution to the controversy."**

The clubs did not have to wait long to come up with a plan to make progress with the authorities, on Wednesday 19th August the clubs met yet again at the Mitre Hotel.[49] All the clubs were represented by two members from each and the discussion we are told was long and heated. At one stage a proposal was made to formally form a Northern Rugby Union. This was defeated as many of the clubs were not prepared to take action which would result in separation. It would seem the clubs still were still clinging to the opinion they were members of the Rugby Union from this statement. The clubs were also opposed to adopting the principles of

---

[48] York Herald 14th August 1895
[49] Hartlepool 20th August 1895

professionalism. Their Lancashire counterparts had no such qualms!

The meeting lasted four hours and at its conclusion the press were informed of the resolution that had been passed by the clubs:-

**"That a sub-committee consisting of five representatives of the late Senior Competition be appointed to meet a like number from the Yorkshire Rugby Union Committee."**

The members of that delegation were Mr. Sewell from Leeds, Mr. Holdsworth from Dewsbury, Mr. Brierley from Batley, Mr. Fattorini from Manningham and Mr. Nicholl from Halifax. The clubs were still trying to dictate to the authorities and bend them to their own will, little wonder the authorities acted in the manner they did.

On that same evening the Yorkshire Committee also met and totally ignored the situation with the senior clubs. They just got on with working through the items on the agenda. They selected the grounds for four early matches in the county championship. They then broke up without receiving any communication from the senior clubs. The reporter did write that:-

**"The future course of the dispute is, therefore, somewhat in doubt, though, as will be seen, a conference with delegates from the other competitions is already arranged for Monday next."**

That meeting referred was of the Yorkshire Rugby Union Football Committee and was to be held at the Green Dragon Hotel, Leeds. To all intents and purposes, it seemed that the two parties were going down the same path they had back in 1892. It was generally believed by the clubs that after a good deal of talking a compromise would be arrived at and all would go back to as it was before the dispute arose. That notion was blown out of the water just two days later when an article in the Hull Daily Mail revealed greater troubles this time for the authorities.[50]

**"Within the week a Northern Rugby League will be an accomplished fact. The clubs will comprise Seniors (Yorkshire and Lancashire), who will sever from the parent body, make their own laws, including payment for broken time. Leeds, Huddersfield, and Bradford, finally deciding whether to join or be thrown decline. The three best of the second competitionists will probably be invited to join, the Yorkshire nine remaining clubs will fill up their card with Lancashire clubs. It is proposed to hold a first senior Lancashire – Yorkshire match the same day as the county match and in close proximity."**

Given this news one must ask the obvious question, namely, what happened from 20th August when the clubs voted not to form a Northern League and 22nd August when we are told that league is more or less an

---

[50] Hull Daily Mail 22nd August 1895

established fact? After all this time we shall perhaps never be able to answer that question particularly as the minutes for the new Northern Union for this period are now missing. There is little possibility that the minutes of these crucial meetings leading up to the split still exist if they were ever written. There is however, in the opinion of the author, one credible scenario that is to some extent supported by evidence.

It would be reasonable to assume that the five people from the senior club delegation would have known members of the football committee that were to meet on 26th August in Leeds. It is also reasonable to assume that informal chats or discussions could have taken place on individual levels, the object being to see just how the land lay for the clubs. That being the case it is the author's belief that the clubs via these delegates were told a number of things that directed their immediate actions.

Firstly, they were told there was no guarantee that the senior clubs would be admitted back into the Yorkshire Rugby Union such was the ill feeling directed toward them by the rest of the county clubs. Secondly, they were told that this ill feeling extended well beyond the county borders and if they were readmitted to the rugby union fold there was no guarantee that any club would want to give them a fixture. It must be remembered that by this time in the year most clubs would have finalised their fixtures for the coming season. If that were not bad enough, they were also informed of a proposition that was to be put to the English Rugby Union. If that proposition were to be passed it would allow all county authorities to audit the books of every club under its jurisdiction. Such a resolution would make it almost impossible to hide broken time payments clubs made to players.

As we shall see later evidence does support these assumptions. Following the meeting on Monday 26th August of the Yorkshire Committee the Leeds Mercury the following day carried a detailed account of the proceedings.[51]

**"The Secretary read the following letter, which he had received from Mr. Holdsworth:-**

**Hollinroyd Wood, Dewsbury, Aug, 20th 1895**

**Dear sir, - Two representatives from each club forming the late Senior Competition met last night to consider their position, and the following resolution was adopted:- That a sub-committee of five members from the late Senior Competition be appointed to meet sub-committee of the Yorkshire Rugby Union, to place before them a scheme for a settlement of the dispute.' I shall be glad to hear from you when it will be convenient, giving about a week's notice, so that our scheme can be fully prepared."**

---

[51] Leeds Mercury 27th August 1895

The letter went on to name the five gentlemen who would represent the clubs. It was proposed by a Mr. Hirst that the committee should receive the delegation and hear just what their scheme and suggestions were. He went on to say he was taking that course of action because there were rumours that a Northern Union was to be formed. He wished to test the genuineness of the professions of a desire to return to the Union. He went on:-

**"If there was any truth in the rumours, the movement must have been going on before the letter he had read was written. For his part, he could not understand how any gentleman could send such a communication as Mr. Holdsworth and yet be in negotiation for the formation of a Northern Union. He thought it best for them to receive the deputation, because if they refused, they might give the dissentient clubs cause to say they had been driven to form a Northern Union because the Yorkshire Rugby Union would not give them a hearing."**

He would see just how prophetic his words would turn out to be just a few days later. The report went on to tell of further discussions:-

**"Mr. Tattersall, who, however, wished to know if the deputation would be received by the whole committee. He had been told by a representative of the Senior Clubs that the gentlemen appointed on behalf of the clubs would not meet the committee, but**

**only a sub-committee of similar number to themselves.**

**Mr Miller thought the letter very unsatisfactory. It did not give any information as to what the deputation wanted to interview them about. So far as he could see there was no difficulty to be overcome beyond the unwillingness of the Senior Clubs to acknowledge they had acted in a rash and hasty manner. If they received a deputation, they could not allow that deputation to impose conditions, nor, if they appeared as representatives of a combination, could they even recognise them. If they came as representatives of individual clubs, they could only point them to the bye-laws to which they must give obedience before they could receive consideration, and even if they wished to complain of anything they had put themselves out of court by their resignation."**

Tattersall went on to say the deputation should have been set up before the clubs resigned, he felt the clubs were playing a game of 'bluff' and they had found the committee holding 'a full hand'. As a result, he could not agree to the resolution but was in favour of finding a solution were that to be possible. He did say that he was strongly opposed to a meeting with the deputation unless it were by the full committee. Other members had their say and expressed the view that the deputation could only be viewed as representing their own clubs. Another stated in an amendment to the original resolution that they should not meet the deputation until the senior clubs accepted the promotion on merit principle passed by the general meeting. The general feeling was the senior clubs would be welcome to return to the fold providing they accepted the ruling of that general committee.

After a great deal of further discussion, the original motion and the amendment were voted upon and passed by a vote of 8 to 2. It was then decided to call a meeting of the full Yorkshire County Rugby Union Committee for Monday September 9th and they would receive the deputation to meet the full committee on that date. The problem with that was quite simple, the meeting was just twelve days before the new season commenced. The senior clubs had no fixtures arranged and should they do nothing prior to the meeting they ran the risk of struggling to get a full fixture list for the coming season. Equally worrying was that more or less the very same committee had refused to set up a sub-committee of five members to meet with them.

The clubs knew that if they appeared before the full committee then the smaller clubs would hold the upper hand on that committee. Equally worrying was the decision that the authorities would only meet the delegation if they were representing their individual clubs. They were not prepared to continence the delegation representing the Senior Competition which now no longer existed. The clubs were still further backed into a corner and it was getting tighter, the authorities were determined to keep them there until they complied with their demands.

In the same issue of the Leeds Mercury there was a report which dealt with the rumours that were flying all over the county. One which would be worrying to the authorities the reporter stated was:-

**"One the one hand, it is freely asserted that the Northern Union is actually formed, and that nine of the twelve Senior clubs are already pledged to join it, in conjunction with leading Lancashire clubs. That may be so, but it is most difficult to obtain any definite statement from responsible parties belonging to those clubs, and it is at least strange that where so much has been positively resolved upon there should be so great a reticence respecting it."**

The reporter went on to perhaps suggest a reason for this reticence, namely that the members of the senior clubs had not been consulted and asked to vote as to whether their club should actually leave the Rugby Union or not. The Leeds club who had been one of the three Yorkshire clubs that had been adamant they did not wish to leave the Rugby Union had decided to put the matter to the members to decide upon. The reporter claiming the club did not have a mandate to leave the Rugby Union. The reporter also revealed that the senior clubs intended holding yet another meeting that evening 27th August and had another planned for 29th August.

It is hard to say just what the situation really was, had the Northern Union already been formed and the delegation was attempting to get the authorities to ratify it without them knowing of the new union? Certainly that would seem to be the case for the reporter told the readers:-

**"The clubs whose action is doubtful are, Leeds, Bradford and Huddersfield, and there is a strong feeling in those organisations against a step which necessitates breaking with the Rugby Union, as the formation of a Northern Union will inevitably compel them to do so, and it is asserted that the other nine, in order to put pressure upon the wavering three, have given them to understand that they must take a definite course by Thursday at the latest, which implies that the Huddersfield meeting will see the new Union launched in definite shape."**

The above would suggest that the clubs had already decided that a new Northern Union would be formed, if that was the case why did they go through the continuing charade with the Yorkshire Rugby Union. If further evidence of this was needed it came from Lancashire where it seemed that Swinton and Salford had reiterated their decision not to join the other clubs and resign from the Lancashire Rugby Union. As we now know they would be joined by the three dissenting Yorkshire outfits leading up to that fateful 29th August date.

The final paragraph of the article is really quite telling:-

**"A gentleman who professes to be in full knowledge of the course of the negotiations that have been carried on, and who is certainly in a position to speak**

**with some confidence, assured our representative that the Northern League will be gone on with even if Bradford, Leeds and Huddersfield do withdraw. He expressed the utmost confidence that their efforts would be attended with success and that ere long any club or clubs at present remaining outside would petition to get in. He stated that the new body proposed to make payment for broken time only; to work, in fact, on the lines which Yorkshire tried hard to secure some months ago. Eight of the clubs are in favour of the League and are determined to go on with it."**

If the clubs were so determined why then continue the nonsense of negotiating with the county authorities? Interestingly on that same Monday evening that the county authorities were meeting so were the Leeds club. At that committee meeting the decision was made to throw in their lot with the new Northern Union. Given the clubs' previous stance opposing such a move, why then the change of heart. Perhaps they accepted the writing on the wall that the county authorities would not move on their decision and the Senior Competition was now dead in the water. The other reason could well have been they knew the Northern Union was already in being and feared being left in limbo if they did not join it and the rugby union did not allow them back into the Union. As was stated earlier that was more than a possibility.

In truth the senior clubs in both counties had not formally resigned from the English Rugby Union at this time even though their actions had not been approved by that body. However, it is a moot point if that really was the case as in order to be a member of the English Rugby Union a club needed to be a member of an affiliated body namely a county union. Some were arguing that this was not the case but OLD EBOR the renowned writer stated that this was indeed the case and by resigning from the county union a club was also resigning from the parent body. He clarified the position when writing in the Athletic News Football Annual for 1895-96:-[52]

**"The Senior Competition for which the leading clubs so tenaciously and successfully fought three years ago has ceased to exist... Unfortunately, the broader view was not taken; the two lowest clubs in the Senior Competition were re-elected and no explanation of the reasons for this course of action and no statement as to the committee's intentions regarding the future were furnished ...**

**But the greatest mistake of all was to resign membership of the Yorkshire Union and to attempt to shelter themselves under the wing of the parent body. Those who advised this step now seem astonished to find that membership of the English Union entails acknowledgement of the County Union's authority. They can perhaps now understand the readiness with which the English Union accepted**

---

[52] The Athletic News Annual 1895-96

**their fees of membership. It seemed a simple act to hand over their subscriptions but in reality, it was handing over every vestige of independence left to them, for it gave the English Union and through that body the Yorkshire Union just the far reaching control which the two latter bodies must in their secret hearts have desired."**

One wonders why if OLD EBOR could see that situation just why the senior clubs could not. It was all getting a little confused for the supporters reading such accounts of events in the newspapers.

What was interesting to note was the subtle change in emphasis by the clubs and consequently the newspaper reports from this time on. The emphasis now was moving away from the dispute the senior clubs had with the authorities with regard to who should have control of the now defunct Senior Competition. In its place was the issue of broken time payments which was beginning to take centre stage for the first time. There is little doubt that the senior clubs in both Yorkshire and Lancashire had been making these payments to players and had done so for many years. Now it seemed they intended to use such payments or the authority's refusal to legalise such payments as a reason for continuing their dispute.

The Hull Daily Mail on 27th August reported that the senior clubs were to meet again that same evening.[53] The report stated that at that meeting the Northern Union

---

[53] Hull Daily Mail 27th August 1895

would formally come into being. It also stated that Bradford and Huddersfield would make a decision as to whether to join the new organisation or remain loyal to the Rugby Union. It was reported that the Bradford players had threatened to leave the club if it did not go with the new organisation. So advanced were the plans by the new organisation the newspaper reported that playing games by the clubs would begin on Saturday 7th September.

The following day the Leeds Mercury carried a lengthy article detailing events at the meeting of the senior clubs at the Mitre Hotel, Leeds. It is pertinent to note that activity by the Lancashire clubs at this time seems to be very muted. Either that or it conducted its meetings in secret as the newspapers carried little or no news of their activities. To all intents and purposes, the Lancashire clubs who had been the driving force initially in the dispute were now content to take a back seat and simply go along with supporting whatever the Yorkshire clubs did. Ironically the Lancashire clubs held a meeting on that same Tuesday evening 27th August and the report of this only appeared on 29th August and then in of all newspaper The Edinburgh Daily News. The report makes interesting reading not because of which clubs attended but those who did not.[54]

**"At a meeting in Manchester on Tuesday night of Oldham, Rochdale Hornets, Tyldesley, Leigh, Wigan,**

---

[54] Edinburgh DailyMail 29th August 1895

**St Helens, Broughton Rangers, Warrington and Widnes, it was agreed unanimously to join in the Northern Rugby Union. The representatives of these clubs will therefore attend the meeting at Huddersfield tonight, fully prepared to act in complete agreement with the Yorkshire clubs. Stockport and one or two other clubs are also expected to join the Union."**

It is interesting to note that yet again the two powerful clubs Salford and Swinton did not attend that meeting and had decided to remain in the Rugby Union fold. *(Both clubs would remain in the rugby union for the 1895-96 season. However, at the end of the season seeing so many of the senior clubs were now in the Northern Union they applied for membership which was granted on 6th June 1896.)* Equally important that meeting was held two days before the famous meeting at the George Hotel and suggests that the Northern Union was already in existence albeit on an informal basis.

When that meeting at the Mitre Hotel began a long discussion was held with regard to the resolution that had been passed at the previous meeting with regard to setting up a delegation of five members. The consensus was that the authority's decision to meet them at a full committee meeting was very unfavourable and the offer should be turned down. In the end the clubs passed the following resolution:-

**"The Yorkshire Rugby Football Union not having seen it advisable to appoint a sub-committee, as desired to meet a deputation of the late Senior Competition, we decide to make no further application on this subject to the above Union."**

This would suggest or even confirm that plans were well advanced for a Northern Union by the clubs. It also clearly showed that the clubs were still trying to dictate to the authorities just what they should do to accommodate them. The reporter went on to state as much when writing that after further discussions the formation of a Northern Union was the way forward. They then hedged their bets somewhat by stating they intended to do so on strictly amateur lines but with the acceptance of 'broken-time payments'. Given the Rugby Union had already charged William Cail just week previously to produce new rules regarding professionalism, there was no chance that the authorities would sanction a Northern Union openly paying broken time.

When a number of the people present at the meeting were questioned by the reporter it can be clearly seen the change in emphasis now adopted by the clubs:-

**"So far as could be gathered from individual expressions of opinion, however, the promoters are averse to launching out upon pure professionalism, and some of them regard their movement as a crusade against the Rugby Union's refusal to accept**

**payment for broken time as a working-class basis rather than as action in any way antagonistic to the rest of Yorkshire."**

It was a very clever shift in emphasis, as it was back in 1893 that Miller and Newsome the Yorkshire representatives had proposed to the Rugby Union at its AGM that broken time payments be approved by the authorities. It was such a desire back then that carried the almost total support of the clubs in the county. It was only by some very dubious proxy votes that the motion was defeated. Now however, in 1895 the senior clubs were attempting to regain that support back from those same clubs who were at odds with the stand they had made when wanting to decide just who if any clubs were to be promoted into the Senior Competition. The new Northern Union was now inevitable and a further meeting was to be held on 29th August at the George Hotel in Huddersfield. It was a meeting which would be attended by the senior club representatives from Lancashire and Yorkshire and would finally formalise the events of the past few months.

Even at this late stage it appeared that Leeds, Bradford and Huddersfield were not the only clubs hesitating about joining the new organisation. Halifax was in the same boat and reports in the newspaper suggested that they along with Bradford were more than just hedging their bets. Both of these clubs in the run up to the George Hotel meeting had been holding their own meetings with the premier association football clubs in the respective towns. Halifax in particular were wanting to amalgamate with the soccer club and ground share. (*As is often said about the sport there is nothing new in rugby league.*)

The Rugby Union also chipped in at this time stating that the new rules on professionalism drawn up by Cail would be voted on at a meeting on 19th September. In a sop to the senior clubs Rowland-Hill the Secretary made the point that the new rules would not be imposed retrospectively. That meant any club that wanted to remain with the Rugby Union would not be punished for any indiscretions prior to that date.

As was stated earlier the clubs were now changing tact and adopting the argument that their dispute with the authorities centred around broken time payments and the Rugby Unions' refusal to sanction them. They added to the confusion to a large extent by also putting forward the argument that the Yorkshire authorities were refusing to meet the delegation from the now defunct Senior Competition clubs. This was not strictly true as the authorities had agreed to meet them at a full committee meeting on 9th September. The point at issue was that the authorities would not accept that delegation as representing all the twelve clubs. What they required was that twelve representatives attend that meeting and apply for reinstatement for their respective clubs.

As we know at 6.30 pm. Thursday 29th August at the George Hotel in Huddersfield twenty one representatives met and formally set up the Northern Rugby Football

Union. We do not know what exactly was said or went on at that meeting as the minutes for the organisation for this period are missing that is if minutes of the meeting were actually taken. What we do know is that the meeting was held in private and afterwards the newspaper reporters were briefed on what had transpired. As ever we are therefore reliant upon the newspaper reports of those events.

At this point It may be prudent to cover the third point that may well have been discussed during the informal talks mentioned earlier between the delegates for the clubs and members of the authorities prior to the meeting on the 26th August. Strangely the evidence initially comes from a New Zealand newspaper Press on 28th November 1895. It was well after the breakaway but in an article very critical of the split by the English clubs the reporter revealed to the reader:-[55]

**"The proposal (submitted to the Annual General Meeting of the Rugby Union) which will empower the County Committees to audit the clubs accounts was probably the last straw which drove the conscience-stricken dissenters into open revolt. It deprived them of any chance of concealing their offences as heretofore by a judicious manipulation of their accounts."**

Whether this was a factor or not we may never know but it does put forward a very powerful argument that clubs

[55] Press 28th November 1895

*Rugby League is Born*

would find it more difficult to hide illegal payments they made to players.

# CHAPTER FIVE

## (The Meeting)

Given that the minutes for the Northern Union for this period in its history are missing it is difficult to say just what the mood was or would have been on that fateful Thursday evening. Was the feeling one of elation that finally all of the plans that had been in the melting pot for months were to finally come to fruition. Or was it a feeling of deflation that in spite of all the efforts they had failed in their endeavour to get the authorities to bend to their will. Consequently, as ever we must rely on the newspaper reports of the day which to some extent could be shaped by the people who attended the meeting telling reporters what they wanted them to know. Most newspapers carried more or less the same account of what went on at the meeting.

At 6.30 pm. The representatives of the twenty one senior clubs from Lancashire and Yorkshire sat down around a conference table. The first order of business was to appoint a chairman for the meeting and that honour went to Mr. Waller from the Brighouse club. Then a secretary was appointed pro-tem and that was Joseph Platt from the Oldham club. There was little doubt he would get the job given he had been a driving force in both counties for the clubs breaking away from the Union. He was also the force behind the drive toward a professional league in Lancashire.

That done all of the representatives present unanimously agree to the official forming of a Northern Rugby Football Union. They made the pledge that they would push forward their new organisation without any delay on the principle of payment for bone-fide broken time payments only. Why that should be was something of a mystery but could well have been to leave the door open to perhaps re-joining the Rugby Union. The meeting had before it a letter of application from the Stockport club and they were admitted into membership of the new Union.

Each of the representatives with the exception of Mr Holdsworth from the Dewsbury club produced a letter of resignation from the English Rugby Union which they handed to Joseph Platt. Holdsworth stating the Dewsbury club needed more time to formally make a decision. They were given until the following Tuesday to decide whether to join the Union or not. That done a sub-committee was then established to consider the rules and bye-laws of the game. The problem was that the Rugby Union had before it the new rules on professionalism that William Cail had drawn up. Many in the game were predicting that the London authorities would not accept the resignation of the clubs but rather they would simply throw the clubs out for being in breach of the new professionalism laws. In addition, they would disallow any other club from playing the rebel clubs or even setting foot on their grounds.

If the clubs held out the opinion that given time the rugby union authorities would come around to their way of thinking and welcome them back into the fold they were to be mistaken. The new rules stated quite clearly that broken time payments were a professional act and so not allowed. It was a view that would strengthen in the coming months and years rather than weaken. The clubs still clung to the belief their suspension from the parent body would be only a temporary one.

The meeting continued with other housekeeping chores which needed to be settled one being an agreement to hold meetings alternately in Leeds and Manchester. The main priority however, was that of arranging fixtures and it was agreed that the club secretaries would meet at the Spread Eagle Hotel, in Manchester on the following Tuesday. At that meeting a fixture list would be drawn up. William Hirst who was the Hon. Secretary of the Yorkshire Rugby Union and that counties representative on the committee of the English Rugby Union resigned both those positions. When interviewed following the meeting he repudiated the idea that the new Union was in any way a professional body. He reiterated the view that broken time payments only would be made to players.

Others present at the meeting told reporters that the bye-laws of the organisation which had been placed before the English Rugby Union were such that it was impossible to break the rules on professionalism. It was a case of an unstoppable force meeting an immovable object with regard to this matter and the clubs view of the situation. What the clubs would not accept was that under the new rules broken time payments constituted professionalism mind you that was the stance they had taken for a long time prior to the meeting. That done the meeting broke up and the new Northern Union was now a reality.

Sadly, not all in the newspaper world saw the new Union in the same light as did the clubs themselves. The Sheffield Daily Telegraph headlined the news 'A PROFESSIONAL UNION DECIDED UPON.' The Western Mail down in Cardiff was even more explicit with its headline 'PROFESSIONALISM AT LAST'. Oven in Lancashire the Manchester Courier carried a similar headline 'PROFESSIONAL UNION DECIDED UPON' the reporter did also mention one problem the fledgeling organisation would have to tackle immediately. It stated that the Lancashire Society of Referees had decided to boycott the new union so if the games were to be played, they would need to find referees prepared to leave the rugby union to officiate at the games.

There was a very prophetic piece in the Sunday Times which time would show to be correct. The reporter was talking of the new season and the effects of professionalism generally in soccer but then specifically the new Northern Union:-[56]

---

[56] Sunday Times 1st September 1895

"The most striking fact that confronts one in connection with the season, however, is supplied by the Northern Rugby clubs, who unable to swallow the new regulations for the prevention of professionalism drafted by the Rugby Union and not seeing their way clear to evade the same, have at last had to stand forth in their true colours. The recently formed Northern Union will keep up the force of professing sympathy with amateurism whilst at the same time recognising the 'broken-time' basis. That is to say, that when a footballer gets tired of earning 7s 6d at his legitimate occupation, he will be able to secure the same by playing. Our Northern friends may not imagine that this amounts to professionalism – but it does all the same."

It is really quite odd that the issue of broken time only came to the fore front around a week or so prior to the meeting at the George Hotel. Now it was being used as the reasons for the breakaway. Gone is any mention of the Lancashire clubs seeking to set up a fully professional league. Equally missing was any mention of the dispute between the Yorkshire clubs and the authorities with regard to 'promotion on merit' and the senior clubs refusing to bow before that particular alter. People like the new secretary Joseph Platt were happy to claim the high moral ground in blaming the Rugby Union for the schism rather than focusing on their own demands on the authorities.

Perhaps the last word is best left to that unnamed reporter from the Sunday Times when he wrote:-

**"How long will the inhabitants of the counties interested be content with purely inter-club competition.**

**Rugby combinations, however, will find they are riding a horse of a different colour. Such attractive fixtures as those versus Blackheath, Cardiff, Newport Gloucester etc. will be taboo."**

That however, is as they say a story for another day.

## CHAPTER SIX

## CONCLUSIONS

The question now is just what does the evidence from the newspaper reports of the time covering these events really tell us. I have no doubt the reader will draw their own conclusions and they will perhaps differ from that of the author. The first thing to be said is that the dispute between the senior clubs and the authorities was not a short-term couple of weeks affair. No, the roots of the dispute lay way back in 1892 rather than in 1895. The second thing is that the myth perpetuated by the early officials of the new organisation, namely the issue was one of broken time payments, being the cause of the split is not entirely correct or even true.

This was certainly not the case; it was only a week or so before the setting up of the Northern Union that broken time indeed came to the fore. The clubs in Lancashire had simply jumped onto the band wagon of broken time to deflect attention away from their prolonged attack on the authorities with regard to a professional league. The clubs at the outset had pushed hard for a fully professional league to be approved by the authorities leading to their resignation from the Lancashire Rugby Union. However, over time they had come to realise such a league was never going to gain approval on so many fronts. This had become apparent following the suspension of Leigh, Salford and Wigan back in 1893-94.

When that happened, they had changed tack and cast envious eyes on the powers the Yorkshire senior clubs had in controlling their own Senior Competition. They saw the Yorkshire outfits as being in control of their own destiny while theirs was in the hands of the Lancashire authorities. The Lancashire authorities were never going to give up control of any aspect of the game, in truth they were unable to do so simply because the English Rugby Union had recently vetoed any such scheme.

In Yorkshire the dispute was a simple one, namely who had the authority to control the Senior Competition. The clubs argued that control had been given to them in 1892 while the authorities felt they had not, claiming such power had only been devolved for the first season of the Senior Competition. The cause of the animosity was purely and simply the issue of 'promotion on merit'. The clubs clearly had shown they were never going to be prepared to consent to any of the twelve clubs suffering relegation. As the clubs were able to re-elect the bottom clubs, they were never going to vote any of their contemporaries out of the Senior Competition. This put them at odds with not only the authorities but most of the clubs in the county.

The authorities were forced to take action and it had been action that was diametrically opposed to that they had taken in 1892. Back then the majority of support had been with the senior clubs not the authorities, now the roles were reversed. Equally the anger felt by smaller junior clubs had caused them to take action and they had simply out manoeuvred the senior clubs. They had done so by voting as a block against any committee nomination at the Yorkshire AGM from a member of any of the senior clubs. Thus, they had greater control of the rugby union committee in the county and they could and would stifle any efforts by the senior clubs to continue defying the authorities.

In efforts to regain the moral high ground the senior clubs had begun to use the issue of broken time payments or more accurately the authority's refusal to sanction such payments as a reason for the dispute. Back in 1893 most clubs in the county had favoured being able to make such payments and the senior clubs were seeking to gain that support once again by referring back to the issue.

This argument also cleverly focused attention on the intransigent attitude the whole of the south of the country had on broken time payments. The clubs were pushing forward the rights of the working man to be entitled to compensation for wages lost because of playing for their club. There was no doubt such claims were relevant and perhaps justified but sadly the clubs really were not interested in the welfare of their players rather the main focus of their attention was on the clubs getting what they wanted. They also set out to perpetuate the belief that the authority's actions had forced them to take the path they had.

The actions of the senior clubs over the previous couple of seasons had provoked the authorities into action with regard to the issue of broken time payments. There could be little doubt about the Rugby Union view with regard to this issue and their action gave the senior clubs no room to manoeuvre. We can see exactly just what William Cail had come up with regarding the new rules on professionalism from an article in the Daily Telegraph the day after the meeting at the George Hotel:-[57]

**"By this code an individual becomes a professional if, amongst a score of other acts, he is found 'Asking, receiving, or relying on a promise, direct or implied, to receive any money consideration whatever, actual or prospective: any employment or advancement: any establishment in business or any compensation whatever for;'**

- a. **Playing football or rendering any service to a football organisation.**
- b. **Training or loss of time connected therewith.**
- c. **Compensation for time lost in playing football or in travelling in connection with football.**
- d. **Expenses in excess of the amount actually disbursed on account of reasonable hotel or travelling expenses."**

One had to wonder just what were the **'scores of other acts'** were that Cail had put into the new rules which were to be voted on in mid-September. One such act was

---

[57] The Daily Telegraph 30th August 1895

that which was mentioned earlier in the New Zealand newspaper regarding the authorities being able to audit any club's books. According to an article in the Hull Daily Mail the new rules professionalised any club, or anyone who did not conform:-[58]

**"Refusing to produce a club's books or documents or to allow its officials to give evidence or to assist in carrying out these rules when requested by the Union to do so."**

There is no doubt that such a rule was not within the spirit of English law but the authorities got away with ordering it. There was no longer any wriggle room regarding broken time payments for the senior clubs given those conditions. Perhaps the clubs had little choice but to do what they did on that Thursday evening.

By the time the meeting on 29th August came around the clubs I believe had already decided to set up a Northern Union if they had not already done so at least a week earlier. The clubs had not for the first time muddied the waters in the dispute with the rugby authorities by making the claim that the authorities had refused to deal with them. Again, this was not true the authorities had stated clearly, they would as a full committee meet the delegation from the clubs. They had also stated that as the Senior Competition no longer existed the five delegates from the clubs could only speak on behalf of

---

[58] Hull Daily Mail 4th September 1895

their respective clubs. This was a far cry from the claim made by the clubs themselves.

So it was under these circumstances that the club representatives gathered at the George Hotel on that Thursday evening. It is hard to see just what other course of action they could have taken given the corner they had backed themselves into by this time. We tend to think that this now famous meeting was a long drawn out affair but was it really. In essence when the representatives met, they firstly formalised the now Northern Rugby Union, in truth it probably had existed informally for some time. That done they all drew up a letter of resignation from the Rugby Union again something that was not necessary as they were no longer members but it did serve to perpetuate the myth. Finally, they agreed to meet once again on the following Tuesday to draw up a fixture list. The truth is those club representatives probably sat down to a good dinner at the hotel by 7.30 pm.

As stated, I think the Northern Union was already agreed upon and the meeting simply ratified the actions taken over the previous weeks and months. The clubs had been paying broken time for years albeit under the counter and could very well have carried on doing so for much longer. That was not the issue rather other more selfish ones were driving the clubs down the path to the split from the Rugby Union.

Finally, there is one hypothetical question that springs to mind regarding that meeting, namely did the clubs think the split they would create was to be a permanent one. Or did they believe that that after a season or two the Rugby Union authorities would alter their stance and allow the clubs to return to the fold under their terms. Whatever the answer to that is we shall never know as the game they created that evening still flourishes to this day. It was however not formed out of a dispute over broken time payments as we are led to believe. Rather it was formed out of the clubs' own self interests and a desire to control their own destiny.

# APPENDIX ONE
# GEORGE BOAK

As the 1893-94 season was approaching the Huddersfield club were looking to strengthen their side. To that end a supposed former committeeman of the club by the name of Hardy learned of two crack three quarters who were playing for one of the top teams in Cumberland. The club was based in the village of Cummersdale and named the Cummersdale Hornets.

The two players were John (Jock) Forsythe and George Boak, Forsythe was a centre while Boak was looked upon as a wingman who possessed that most precious commodity, speed. The pair were looked upon as the best two three quarters in Cumberland at the time. Boak was born in 1870 so when the Huddersfield club came calling, he was just twenty two years old. That said he was married to Isabella and was the father of three small children and was working in the local Dye Works in the village. The offer made by Huddersfield was too good to refuse even though it was probably in breach of the rugby union rules on professionalism.

Both he and Forsythe left Cummersdale in a hurry, so quickly that they were actually summonsed to appear in the court in Carlisle for leaving their place of work without working the proper notice. Boak was fined and ordered to pay damages to the Dye Works as was Forsythe. Both were given a pre-paid train ticket from Carlisle to Huddersfield which again was against the rules and within a couple of days of arriving at the club Boak was given employment at Read Holiday and Sons a chemical works in Huddersfield. Again, an event that was against the professional rules at the time.

He had though been forced to leave Isabella and his children behind in Carlisle. But such was his reputation and that of Forsythe that the club made a huge decision to alter the style of rugby they were to play that season. At the time in 1893 almost all clubs played with just three three-quarters and with a forward pack consisting of nine men. Some clubs however were now beginning to pull one of the forwards out of the pack and play them in the backs thus playing with four three quarters.

The problem was that even as the players began training with their new club trouble was brewing and it was coming from back in Cumberland and the Cummersdale Hornets club. They claimed that the Yorkshire outfit had enticed the two star players to Huddersfield by offering them incentives and by so doing had professionalised the players. The club also made the claim that Huddersfield were in breach of the laws on professionalism in enticing the players away from the Hornets.

It was Saturday, 2nd September 1893 that we see first mention of the pair when they took part in a practice match. A team of fifteen played against a team of eighteen in order that the selectors could assess the form of the players. The local newspaper reported that Boak and Forsythe had turned out but made no mention of their performances. There was no doubt they were going to play in the first team given the trouble and expense the club had gone to bring them to Yorkshire.

They played their first official game for the club the following Saturday, 9th September against Hunslet which was drawn. The Yorkshire Evening Post reported:-[59]

**"Huddersfield adopted the system of four three quarters, the new men being Forsythe and Boak."**

While both players got a brief mention in the match report the thrust of the article was that Huddersfield by playing with four three quarters suffered badly in the scrum. Hunslet seemed to dominate possession thus starving the two newcomers of the ball. It did not auger well for the season that was now upon the game.

---

[59] Yorkshire Evening Post 11th September 1893

Sadly, it did not get any better for the club or the players the following week, 16th September they lost this time to Bradford. Once again, their forwards being one short in the pack were overwhelmed and possession was in short supply for Boak and his mate. By the middle of the following week, it was reported in the local newspapers that the Cumberland club had written to the Yorkshire authorities officially stating their claims. They had also complained to their parent body in Cumberland. Boak continued to play and the club met Dewsbury on 23rd September and suffered yet another loss. There followed losses to both Hull and Manningham. While all of this was going on a meeting had been held to address the claims by the Cumberland club. It was not going well for the Huddersfield club who claimed it was a former committeeman who had made the initial approach to both players. The problem was a simple one it was they who had supplied the train tickets and found employment for the players. Eventually the ruling was made that Boak and Forsythe were suspended for being professionals. Also, the club was guilty and suspended until the end of the year.

The claim is made that Boak was therefore the first ever player to be suspended for professionalism in the country if not the world. *(Sadly, that is not the case that dubious honour goes to the Wakefield Trinity player Charles Edward Bartram. Back in the day he was perhaps the best centre in the game and was playing for Harrogate. Wakefield lured him to the club and in 1881 appointed him the assistant secretary of the club. The problem was no such job existed or was needed. Rumours abounded with regard to Bartram's status and he was never to play for England as a result. In 1889 he was banned by the rugby union authorities after it was proved he had accepted a loan from the club. Thus, it is Bartram who was the first player in the world banned over charges of professionalism.)* Boak had played just five games for Huddersfield before being forced to return home to Cumberland and his wife and family. Back home he was to become a publican in Carlisle and he and Isabella would go on to have twelve children of which ten survived. There has been a suggestion that Boak later was reinstated by the Rugby Union but the author found no evidence to support the claim. We do know he ran in 100 yard races and also 130 yard races. Given the latter distance was one used a great deal for professional sprint races at the time it is hard to see that he could be classed as an amateur.

There was also a claim that when the Northern Union was established in 1895 Boak actually returned to the Huddersfield club and began playing once more. Examination of the Huddersfield player register and accounts of matches played at this time have no reference to Boak taking the field. It seems that Forsythe did actually return and play for the club for a number of seasons.

Sadly, things did not end well for Boak, it was claimed by his descendants much later that he became quite depressed toward the end of his life. Sadly, in 1914 he was reported to have been drown in an accident in the River Eden in Carlisle Park. The coroner on investigating the circumstances reportedly came to the conclusion that the evidence was unclear and recorded an open verdict. Boak was just forty three years old when he died.

Many in the game would claim that it was the professionalisation of Boak and Forsythe by the authorities that ultimately was to lead to the disputes covered in this book. The reader must draw their own conclusions with regard to that viewpoint.

Much of the information above was gleaned from the Huddersfield Rugby League Heritage site and was contained in a video of Boak's grandson who was speaking of his recollections of his grandfather.

# APPENDIX TWO

# THE SENIOR COMPETITION SHIELD

When the Senior Competition began the clubs along with the Yorkshire authorities proposed to provide a trophy which was to be presented to the champion club. What they came up with was a magnificent shield as shown below. The first holders of the shield were Bradford who won the Senior Competition championship in that first 1892-93 season. In its last season the Senior Competition was won by Liversedge who pipped Manningham for top spot.

Ironically when the split came in August of 1895 the senior clubs held onto the shield and actually used it as the trophy for the winners of the new Northern Union. Fittingly it was a Yorkshire club, Manningham that were the winners of the competition so the shield had no need to leave the white rose county.

Research has failed to uncover just who manufactured this magnificent embossed shield but one man could well be responsible. That man was Tony Fattorini a member of the Manningham club at the time. His company were to manufacture both the FA Cup and the Rugby League Challenge Cup in later years along with a World Cup trophy. Certainly, the company of Fattorini and Sons has had a long association with rugby league and produced many of the medals that have been presented to players over the years.

*Rugby League is Born*

**THE YORKSHIRE SENIOR COMPETITION CHAMPIONSHIP SHIELD**

# APPENDIX THREE
# TONY FATTORINI

The company of Fattorini and Sons was involved with the Bradford based Manningham Rugby Club prior to the breakaway. Tony Fattorini was at the very centre of the events that were to lead to the formation of the Northern Rugby Union in August 1895. When the Manningham clubs' fortunes declined it switched to the rival code of Association Football. Once again Tony Fattorini was heavily involved in the switch of allegiance that saw Manningham Northern Union club become Bradford City in 1903.

Printed in Great Britain
by Amazon